Praise for *Kubernetes Cookbook*

The best infrastructure is the infrastructure you don't see. The *Kubernetes Cookbook* helps move in that direction. This book provides concrete examples of how to get stuff done so you can get back to your real job. Along the way, you'll build a skill set that helps you take your Kubernetes game to the next level.

—Joe Beda
CTO and Founder of Heptio,
Kubernetes Founder

The *Kubernetes Cookbook* is a fantastic hands-on guide to building and running applications on Kubernetes. It is a great reference and a great way to help you learn to build cloud-native containerized applications.

—Clayton Coleman
Red Hat

In this Cookbook, Sebastien and Michael collect together a number of useful recipes to get you going with Kubernetes, fast. They surface dozens of helpful hints and tips that will get readers hands-on with practical aspects of installing Kubernetes and using it to run applications.

—Liz Rice
Chief Technology Evangelist,
Aqua Security

D1472147

Kubernetes Cookbook
Building Cloud-Native Applications

Sébastien Goasguen and Michael Hausenblas

Beijing · Boston · Farnham · Sebastopol · Tokyo

Kubernetes Cookbook

by Sébastien Goasguen and Michael Hausenblas

Copyright © 2018 Sebastien Goasguen and Michael Hausenblas. All rights reserved.

Published by O'Reilly Media, Inc., 1005 Gravenstein Highway North, Sebastopol, CA 95472.

O'Reilly books may be purchased for educational, business, or sales promotional use. Online editions are also available for most titles (*http://oreilly.com/safari*). For more information, contact our corporate/institutional sales department: 800-998-9938 or *corporate@oreilly.com*.

Editor: Angela Rufino
Production Editor: Colleen Cole
Copyeditor: Rachel Head
Proofreader: Gillian McGarvey

Indexer: Ellen Troutman
Interior Designer: David Futato
Cover Designer: Randy Comber
Illustrator: Rebecca Demarest

March 2018:   First Edition

Revision History for the First Edition
2018-02-14:   First Release

See *http://oreilly.com/catalog/errata.csp?isbn=9781491979686* for release details.

978-1-491-97968-6

[LSI]

For my boys, whose smiles, hugs, and spirits make me a better person.
For my wife with whom I am taking this journey through life.

Sébastien

For Saphira, Ranya, Iannis, and Anneliese.

Michael

Table of Contents

Preface

Welcome to *Kubernetes Cookbook*, and thanks for choosing it! With this book, we want to help you solve concrete problems around Kubernetes. We've compiled over 80 recipes covering topics such as setting up a cluster, managing containerized workloads using Kubernetes API objects, using storage primitives, security configurations, and extending Kubernetes itself. Whether you are very new to Kubernetes or have been using it for a while, we hope that you'll find something useful here to improve your experience and use of Kubernetes.

Who Should Read This Book

You're a developer going cloud-native, or a sysadmin, or maybe you've even found yourself in one of the newfangled DevOps roles? This book will help you navigate your way successfully through the Kubernetes jungle, from development to production. These recipes are not organized in a linear progression of the basic Kubernetes concepts; however, each chapter contains recipes that utilize core Kubernetes concepts and API primitives.

Why We Wrote This Book

Both of us have been using and contributing to Kubernetes for a few years and have seen the many issues beginners and even more advanced users run into. We wanted to share the knowledge we've gathered running Kubernetes in production, as well as developing on and in Kubernetes—i.e., contributing to the core codebase or the ecosystem and writing applications that run on Kubernetes.

Navigating This Book

This cookbook contains 14 chapters. Each chapter is composed of recipes written in the standard O'Reilly recipe format (Problem, Solution, Discussion). You can read this book from front to back or skip to a specific chapter or recipe. Each recipe is independent of the others, and when an understanding of concepts from other recipes are needed, appropriate references are provided. The index is also an extremely powerful resource because sometimes a recipe is also showcasing a specific command and the index highlights these connections.

A Note on Kubernetes Releases

At the time of writing, Kubernetes 1.7 was the latest stable version, released at the end of June 2017, and this is the version we're using throughout the book as the baseline.[1] However, the solutions presented here should, in general, work for older releases, at least down to Kubernetes 1.4; we will call it out explicitly if this is not the case, mentioning the minimum required version.

The Kubernetes release cadence as of 2017 is such that every quarter a new (minor or dot) release is cut; for example, 1.6 was released in March, 1.7 in June, 1.8 in September, and 1.9 in December, as this book was entering production. The Kubernetes release versioning guidelines indicate that you can expect support for a feature for three minor releases at a time.[2] This means that the stable API objects in the 1.7 release will be supported until at least March 2018. However, because the recipes in this book most often only use stable APIs, if you use a newer Kubernetes release, the recipes should still work.

Technology You Need to Understand

This intermediate-level book requires a minimal understanding of a few development and system administration concepts. Before diving into the book, you might want to review the following:

bash (Unix shell)
>   This is the default Unix shell on Linux and macOS. Familiarity with the Unix shell, such as for editing files, setting file permissions and user priveleges, moving files around the filesystem, and doing some basic shell programming, will be beneficial. For a general introduction, consult books such as Cameron Newham's *Learning the bash Shell* or JP Vossen and Carl Albing's *bash Cookbook*, both from O'Reilly.

---

1 "Kubernetes 1.7: Security Hardening, Stateful Application Updates and Extensibility" (*http://blog.kubernetes.io/2017/06/kubernetes-1.7-security-hardening-stateful-application-extensibility-updates.html*).

2 "Kubernetes API and Release Versioning" (*https://github.com/eBay/Kubernetes/blob/master/docs/design/versioning.md*).

Package management

The tools in this book often have multiple dependencies that need to be met by installing some packages. Knowledge of the package management system on your machine is therefore required. It could be *apt* on Ubuntu/Debian systems, *yum* on CentOS/RHEL systems, or *port* or *brew* on macOS. Whatever it is, make sure that you know how to install, upgrade, and remove packages.

Git

Git has established itself as the standard for distributed version control. If you are already familiar with CVS and SVN but have not yet used Git, you should. *Version Control with Git* by Jon Loeliger and Matthew McCullough (O'Reilly) is a good place to start. Together with Git, the GitHub website (*http://github.com*) is a great resource to get started with a hosted repository of your own. To learn about GitHub, check out *http://training.github.com* and the associated interactive tutorial (*http://try.github.io*).

Python

In addition to programming with C/C++ or Java, we always encourage students to pick up a scripting language of their choice. Perl used to rule the world, while these days, Ruby and Go seem to be prevalent. Most examples in this book use Python, but there are a few examples with Ruby, and one even uses Clojure. O'Reilly offers an extensive collection of books on Python, including *Introducing Python* by Bill Lubanovic, *Programming Python* by Mark Lutz, and *Python Cookbook* by David Beazley and Brian K. Jones.

Go

Kubernetes is written in Go. Over the last couple of years, Go has established itself as the new programming language of choice in many startups and for many systems-related open source projects. This cookbook is not about Go programming, but it shows how to compile a few Go projects. Some minimal understanding of how to set up a Go workspace will be handy. If you want to know more, a good place to start is the O'Reilly video training course "Introduction to Go Programming".

Online Resources

Kubernetes manifests, code examples, and other scripts used in this book are available on GitHub (*https://github.com/k8s-cookbook/recipes*). You can clone this repository, go to the relevant chapter and recipe, and use the code as is:

```
$ git clone https://github.com/k8s-cookbook/recipes
```

> The examples in this repo are not meant to represent optimized setups to be used in production. They give you the basic minimum required to run the examples in the recipes.

Conventions Used in This Book

The following typographical conventions are used in this book:

Italic
> Indicates new terms, URLs, email addresses, filenames, and file extensions.

`Constant width`
> Used for program listings, as well as within paragraphs to refer to program elements such as variable or function names, databases, data types, environment variables, statements, and keywords. Also used for commands and command-line output.

`Constant width bold`
> Shows commands or other text that should be typed literally by the user.

`Constant width italic`
> Shows text that should be replaced with user-supplied values or by values determined by context.

> This element signifies a tip or suggestion.

> This element signifies a general note.

> This element indicates a warning or caution.

Using Code Examples

This book is here to help you get your job done. In general, if example code is offered with this book, you may use it in your programs and documentation. You do not need to contact us for permission unless you're reproducing a significant portion of the code. For example, writing a program that uses several chunks of code from this book does not require permission. Selling or distributing a CD-ROM of examples from O'Reilly books does require permission. Answering a question by citing this book and quoting example code does not require permission. Incorporating a significant amount of example code from this book into your product's documentation does require permission.

We appreciate, but do not require, attribution. An attribution usually includes the title, author, publisher, and ISBN. For example: "*Kubernetes Cookbook* by Sébastien Goasguen and Michael Hausenblas (O'Reilly). Copyright 2018 Sébastien Goasguen and Michael Hausenblas, 978-1-491-97968-6."

If you feel your use of code examples falls outside fair use or the permission given above, feel free to contact us at *permissions@oreilly.com*.

O'Reilly Safari

 *Safari* (formerly Safari Books Online) is a membership-based training and reference platform for enterprise, government, educators, and individuals.

Members have access to thousands of books, training videos, Learning Paths, interactive tutorials, and curated playlists from over 250 publishers, including O'Reilly Media, Harvard Business Review, Prentice Hall Professional, Addison-Wesley Professional, Microsoft Press, Sams, Que, Peachpit Press, Adobe, Focal Press, Cisco Press, John Wiley & Sons, Syngress, Morgan Kaufmann, IBM Redbooks, Packt, Adobe Press, FT Press, Apress, Manning, New Riders, McGraw-Hill, Jones & Bartlett, and Course Technology, among others.

For more information, please visit *http://oreilly.com/safari*.

How to Contact Us

Please address comments and questions concerning this book to the publisher:

O'Reilly Media, Inc.
1005 Gravenstein Highway North
Sebastopol, CA 95472

800-998-9938 (in the United States or Canada)
707-829-0515 (international or local)
707-829-0104 (fax)

We have a web page for this book where we list errata, examples, and any additional information. You can access this page at *http://bit.ly/kubernetes-cookbook*.

To comment or ask technical questions about this book, send email to *bookquestions@oreilly.com*.

For more information about our books, courses, conferences, and news, see our website at *http://www.oreilly.com*.

Find us on Facebook: *http://facebook.com/oreilly*

Follow us on Twitter: *http://twitter.com/oreillymedia*

Watch us on YouTube: *http://www.youtube.com/oreillymedia*

Acknowledgments

Thank you to the entire Kubernetes community for developing such amazing software and for being a great bunch of people—open, kind, and always ready to help.

Writing this book turned out to be a much longer project than it should have been, but it is now finished and we are thankful to all the people who helped us. We are particularly in debt to the thorough reviews from Ihor Dvoretski, Liz Rice, and Ben Hall, who helped fix a good number of issues and suggested better organization and recipes that will help all readers.

## CHAPTER 1

Getting Started with Kubernetes

In this first chapter we present recipes that will help you get started with Kubernetes. We show you how to use Kubernetes without installing it and introduce components such as the command-line interface (CLI) and the dashboard, which allow you to interact with a cluster, as well as Minikube, an all-in-one solution you can run on your laptop.

1.1 Using Kubernetes Without Installation

Problem

You want to try Kubernetes without installing it.

Solution

To use Kubernetes without installing it, follow the interactive tutorial on the Kubernetes website (*https://kubernetes.io/docs/tutorials/kubernetes-basics/*).

You can also use the Kubernetes playground (*https://www.katacoda.com/courses/kubernetes/playground*) on Katacoda. Once you're signed in with GitHub or one of the social media authentication methods, you will see the page depicted in Figure 1-1.

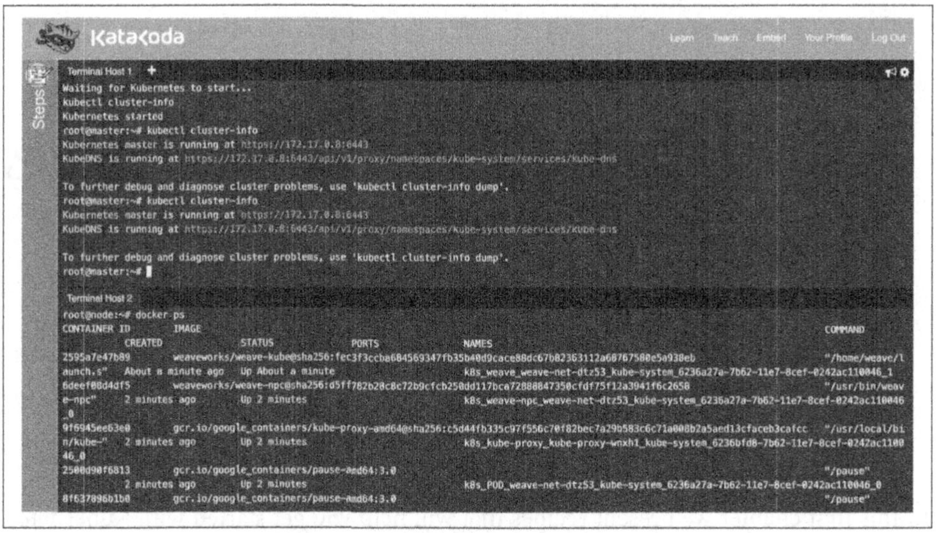

Figure 1-1. Screenshot of the Katacoda Kubernetes playground

Note that an environment you launch in the playground is only available for a limited time—currently one hour—but it's free of charge and all you need is a browser.

1.2 Installing the Kubernetes CLI, kubectl

Problem

You want to install the Kubernetes command-line interface so you can interact with your Kubernetes cluster.

Solution

Install kubectl in one of the following ways:

- Download the source tarballs.
- Use a package manager.
- Build from source (see Recipe 13.1).

The documentation (*https://kubernetes.io/docs/tasks/kubectl/install/*) highlights a few mechanisms to get kubectl. The easiest is to download the latest official release. For example, on a Linux system, to get the latest stable version, enter:

```
$ curl -LO https://storage.googleapis.com/kubernetes-release/release/ \
    $(curl -s https://storage.googleapis.com/kubernetes-release/ \
    release/stable.txt) \
    /bin/linux/amd64/kubectl
```

```
$ chmod +x ./kubectl
```

```
$ sudo mv ./kubectl /usr/local/bin/kubectl
```

Users of macOS can get kubectl simply via Homebrew:

```
$ brew install kubectl
```

Google Kubernetes Engine users (see Recipe 2.7) will get kubectl as part of the gcloud command installation. For example, on Sébastien's local machine:

```
$ which kubectl
/Users/sebgoa/google-cloud-sdk/bin/kubectl
```

Also note that the latest versions of Minikube (see Recipe 1.3) packages kubectl and will install it in your $PATH if it is not found.

Before you move on from this recipe, make sure you have a working kubectl by listing its version. This command will also try to get the version of the default Kubernetes cluster:

```
$ kubectl version
Client Version: version.Info{Major:"1", \
                             Minor:"7", \
                             GitVersion:"v1.7.0", \
                             GitCommit:"fff5156...", \
                             GitTreeState:"clean", \
                             BuildDate:"2017-03-28T16:36:33Z", \
                             GoVersion:"go1.7.5", \
                             Compiler:"gc", \
                             Platform:"darwin/amd64"}
...
```

See Also

- Documentation on installing kubectl (*https://kubernetes.io/docs/tasks/kubectl/ install/*)

1.3 Installing Minikube to Run a Local Kubernetes Instance

Problem

You want to use Kubernetes for testing or development or for training purposes on your local machine.

Solution

Use Minikube. Minikube is a tool that lets you use Kubernetes on your local machine without any installation except for the `minikube` binary. It takes advantage of your local hypervisor (e.g., VirtualBox, KVM) and launches a virtual machine that runs Kubernetes in a single node.

To install the Minikube CLI locally, you can get the latest release or build from source. To get the v0.18.0 release and install `minikube` on a Linux-based machine, do:

```
$ curl -Lo minikube https://storage.googleapis.com/minikube/releases/v0.18.0/ \
                  minikube-linux-amd64

$ chmod +x minikube

$ sudo mv minikube /usr/local/bin/
```

This will put the `minikube` binary in your path and make it accessible from everywhere.

Discussion

Once `minikube` is installed, you can verify the version that is running with the following command:

```
$ minikube version
minikube version: v0.18.0
```

You can start it with:

```
$ minikube start
```

Once the startup phase has finished, your Kubernetes client, `kubectl`, will have a `minikube` context and will automatically start using this context. Checking what nodes you have in your cluster will return the `minikube` hostname:

```
$ kubectl get nodes
NAME       STATUS   AGE
minikube   Ready    5d
```

See Also

- Minikube documentation (*https://kubernetes.io/docs/getting-started-guides/mini kube/*)

- `minikube` source on GitHub (*https://github.com/kubernetes/minikube*)

1.4 Using Minikube Locally for Development

Problem

You want to use Minikube locally for testing and development of your Kubernetes application. You have installed and started minikube (see Recipe 1.3) and want to know a few extra commands to simplify your development experience.

Solution

The Minikube CLI offers a few commands that make your life easier. The CLI has built-in help that you can use to discover the subcommands on your own—here's a snippet:

```
$ minikube
...
Available Commands:
  addons          Modify minikube's kubernetes addons.
...
  start           Starts a local kubernetes cluster.
  status          Gets the status of a local kubernetes cluster.
  stop            Stops a running local kubernetes cluster.
  version         Print the version of minikube.
```

Aside from start, stop, and delete, you should become familiar with the ip, ssh, dashboard, and docker-env commands.

 Minikube runs a Docker engine to be able to start containers. In order to access this Docker engine from your local machine using your local Docker client, you'll need to set up the correct Docker environment with minikube docker-env.

Discussion

The minikube start command starts the virtual machine (VM) that will run Kubernetes locally. By default it will allocate 2 GB of RAM, so when you are done, do not forget to stop it with minikube stop. Also, you can give the VM more memory and CPUs as well as pick a certain Kubernetes version to run—for example:

```
$ minikube start --cpus=4 --memory=4000 --kubernetes-version=v1.7.2
```

For debugging the Docker daemon that is used inside Minikube, you might find minikube ssh handy; it will log you into the virtual machine. To get the IP address of the Minikube VM, use minikube ip. Finally, to launch the Kubernetes dashboard in your default browser, use minikube dashboard.

If for any reason your Minikube becomes unstable, or you want to start afresh, you can remove it with `minikube stop` and `minikube delete`. Then a `minikube start` will give you a fresh installation.

1.5 Starting Your First Application on Minikube

Problem

You've started Minikube (see Recipe 1.3), and now you want to launch your first application on Kubernetes.

Solution

As an example, you can start the Ghost (*https://ghost.org*) microblogging platform on Minikube using two `kubectl` commands:

```
$ kubectl run ghost --image=ghost:0.9
$ kubectl expose deployments ghost --port=2368 --type=NodePort
```

Monitor the pod manually to see when it starts running and then use the `minikube service` command to open your browser automatically and access Ghost:

```
$ kubectl get pods
NAME                      READY   STATUS    RESTARTS   AGE
ghost-8449997474-kn86m    1/1     Running   0          2h

$ minikube service ghost
```

Discussion

The `kubectl run` command is called a *generator*; it is a convenience command to create a `Deployment` object (see Recipe 4.4). The `kubectl expose` command is also a generator, a convenience command to create a `Service` object (see Recipe 5.1) that routes network traffic to the containers started by your deployment.

1.6 Accessing the Dashboard in Minikube

Problem

You are using Minikube and want to access the Kubernetes dashboard to start your first application from a graphical user interface.

Solution

You can open the Kubernetes dashboard from Minikube with:

```
$ minikube dashboard
```

Click on the plus sign (+) at the top right of the UI that opens in your browser, and you will see the page depicted in Figure 1-2.

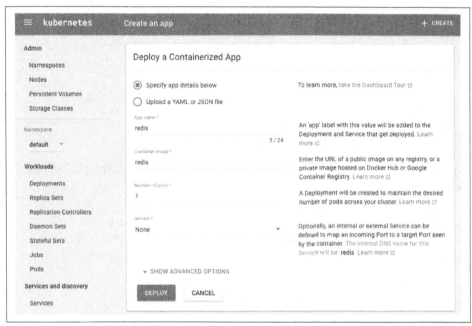

Figure 1-2. Snapshot of the dashboard application create view

Discussion

To create an application, click the Create button in the top-right corner, give the application a name, and specify the Docker image that you want to use. Then click the Deploy button and you will be presented with a new view that shows deployments and replica sets, and after a bit of time you will see a pod. These are some key API primitives we will deal with in greater detail in the rest of the book.

The snapshot in Figure 1-3 presents a typical dashboard view after having created a single application using the Redis container.

Figure 1-3. A dashboard overview with a Redis application

If you go back to a terminal session and use the command-line client, you will see the same thing:

```
$ kubectl get pods,rs,deployments
NAME                            READY     STATUS    RESTARTS   AGE
po/redis-3215927958-4x88v       1/1       Running   0          24m

NAME                    DESIRED   CURRENT   READY     AGE
rs/redis-3215927958     1         1         1         24m

NAME             DESIRED   CURRENT   UP-TO-DATE   AVAILABLE   AGE
deploy/redis     1         1         1            1           24m
```

Your Redis pod will be running the Redis server, as the following logs show:

```
$ kubectl logs redis-3215927958-4x88v
...
```

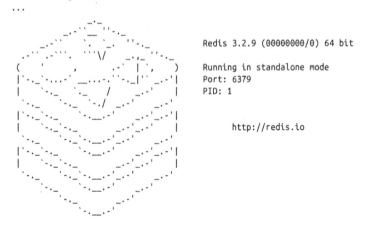

```
Redis 3.2.9 (00000000/0) 64 bit

Running in standalone mode
Port: 6379
PID: 1


        http://redis.io
```

```
...
1:M 14 Jun 07:28:56.637 # Server started, Redis version 3.2.9
1:M 14 Jun 07:28:56.643 * The server is now ready to accept connections on
port 6379
```

## CHAPTER 2

Creating a Kubernetes Cluster

In this chapter we discuss multiple ways to set up a full-blown Kubernetes cluster. We cover low-level, standardized tooling (kubeadm) that also serves as the basis for other installers and show you where to find the relevant binaries for the control plane, as well as for worker nodes. We discuss a containerized Kubernetes setup with hyper kube, demonstrate how to write systemd unit files to supervise Kubernetes components, and finally show how to set up clusters in Google Cloud and on Azure.

2.1 Installing kubeadm to Create a Kubernetes Cluster

Problem

You want to use kubeadm to bootstrap a Kubernetes cluster from scratch.

Solution

Download the kubeadm CLI tool from the Kubernetes package repository.

You will need kubeadm installed on all the servers that will be part of your Kubernetes cluster—not only the master, but also all the nodes.

For example, if you are using Ubuntu-based hosts, on each host do the following as root to set up the Kubernetes package repository:

```
# apt-get update && apt-get install -y apt-transport-https

# curl -s https://packages.cloud.google.com/apt/doc/apt-key.gpg | apt-key add -

# cat <<EOF >/etc/apt/sources.list.d/kubernetes.list
  deb http://apt.kubernetes.io/ kubernetes-xenial main
  EOF
```

```
# apt-get update
```

Now you can install the Docker engine and the various Kubernetes tools. You will need the following:

- The kubelet binary
- The kubeadm CLI
- The kubectl client
- kubernetes-cni, the Container Networking Interface (CNI) plug-in

Install them with:

```
# apt-get install -y docker.io
# apt-get install -y kubelet kubeadm kubectl kubernetes-cni
```

Discussion

Once all the binaries and tools are installed, you are ready to start bootstrapping your Kubernetes cluster. On your master node, initialize the cluster with:

```
# kubeadm init
[kubeadm] WARNING: kubeadm is in beta, please do not use it for production
clusters.
[init] Using Kubernetes version: v1.7.8
[init] Using Authorization modes: [Node RBAC]
[preflight] Running pre-flight checks
...
```

At the end of the initialization, you will be given a command to execute on all your worker nodes (see Recipe 2.2). This command uses a token autogenerated by the initialization process.

See Also

- Using kubeadm to Create a Cluster (*https://kubernetes.io/docs/setup/independent/create-cluster-kubeadm/*)

2.2 Bootstrapping a Kubernetes Cluster Using kubeadm

Problem

You have initialized your Kubernetes master node (see Recipe 2.1) and now need to add worker nodes to your cluster.

Solution

With the Kubernetes package repository configured and `kubeadm` installed as shown in Recipe 2.1, run the `join` command using the token given to you when running the `init` step on the master node:

```
$ kubeadm join --token <token>
```

Head back to your master terminal session and you will see your nodes join:

```
$ kubectl get nodes
```

Discussion

The final step is to create a network that satisfies the Kubernetes networking requirements—especially the single IP address per pod. You can use any of the network add-ons.[1] Weave Net,[2] for example, can be installed on Kubernetes clusters v1.6.0 and above with a single `kubectl` command, like so:

```
$ export kubever=$(kubectl version | base64 | tr -d '\n')
$ kubectl apply -f "https://cloud.weave.works/k8s/net?k8s-version=$kubever"
```

This command will create daemon sets (see Recipe 7.3) running on all nodes in the cluster. These daemon sets use the host network and a CNI (*https://github.com/containernetworking/cni*) plug-in to configure the local node network. Once the network is in place, your cluster nodes will enter the READY state.

For other networking add-ons that you can use to create a pod network during the bootstrapping process with `kubeadm`, see the documentation (*https://kubernetes.io/docs/setup/independent/create-cluster-kubeadm/#pod-network*).

See Also

- Documentation on creating a cluster with `kubeadm` (*https://kubernetes.io/docs/setup/independent/create-cluster-kubeadm/*)

2.3 Downloading a Kubernetes Release from GitHub

Problem

You want to download an official Kubernetes release instead of compiling from source.

---

1 Kubernetes, "Installing Addons" (*https://kubernetes.io/docs/concepts/cluster-administration/addons/*).

2 Weaveworks, "Integrating Kubernetes via the Addon" (*https://www.weave.works/docs/net/latest/kube-addon/*).

Solution

You can follow a manual process and go to the GitHub releases page (*https://github.com/kubernetes/kubernetes/releases*). Choose the release, or potentially prerelease that you want to download. Then choose the source bundle you will need to compile, or download the *kubernetes.tar.gz* file.

Alternatively, you can check the latest release tags using the GitHub API, as shown here:

```
$ curl -s https://api.github.com/repos/kubernetes/kubernetes/releases | \
      jq -r .[].assets[].browser_download_url
https://github.com/kubernetes/kubernetes/releases/download/v1.9.0/
      kubernetes.tar.gz
https://github.com/kubernetes/kubernetes/releases/download/v1.9.0-beta.2/
      kubernetes.tar.gz
https://github.com/kubernetes/kubernetes/releases/download/v1.8.5/
      kubernetes.tar.gz
https://github.com/kubernetes/kubernetes/releases/download/v1.9.0-beta.1/
      kubernetes.tar.gz
https://github.com/kubernetes/kubernetes/releases/download/v1.7.11/
      kubernetes.tar.gz
...
```

Then download the *kubernetes.tar.gz* release package of your choice. For example, to get v1.7.11, do:

```
$ wget https://github.com/kubernetes/kubernetes/releases/download/ \
      v1.7.11/kubernetes.tar.gz
```

If you want to compile Kubernetes from source, see Recipe 13.1.

 Do not forget to verify the secure hash of the *kubernetes.tar.gz* archive. The SHA256 hash is listed on the GitHub release page. After downloading the archive locally, generate the hash and compare it. Even though the release is not signed with GPG, verifying the hash will check the integrity of the archive.

2.4 Downloading Client and Server Binaries

Problem

You have downloaded a release archive (see Recipe 2.3), but it does not contain the actual binaries.

Solution

To keep the size of the release archive small, it does not contain the release binaries. You need to download them separately. To do so, run the *get-kube-binaries.sh* script as shown here:

```
$ tar -xvf kubernetes.tar.gz
$ cd kubernetes/cluster
$ ./get-kube-binaries.sh
```

Once complete, you will have the client binaries in *client/bin*:

```
$ tree ./client/bin
./client/bin
├── kubectl
└── kubefed
```

and the server binaries in *server/kubernetes/server/bin*:

```
$ tree server/kubernetes/server/bin
server/kubernetes/server/bin
├── cloud-controller-manager
├── kube-apiserver
...
```

 If you want to skip downloading the release and quickly download the client and/or server binaries, you can get them directly from *https://dl.k8s.io*. For example, to get the v1.7.11 binaries for Linux, do:

```
$ wget https://dl.k8s.io/v1.7.11/ \
\kubernetes-client-linux-amd64.tar.gz
```

```
$ wget https://dl.k8s.io/v1.7.11/ \
kubernetes-server-linux-amd64.tar.gz
```

2.5 Using a hyperkube Image to Run a Kubernetes Master Node with Docker

Problem

You want to create a Kubernetes master node using a few Docker containers. Specifically, you want to run the API server, scheduler, controller, and etcd key/value store within containers.

Solution

You can use the hyperkube binary plus an etcd container. hyperkube is an all-in-one binary available as a Docker image. You can use it to start all the Kubernetes processes.

To create a Kubernetes cluster, you need a storage solution to keep the cluster state. In Kubernetes, this solution is a distributed key/value store called etcd; therefore, first you need to start an etcd instance. You can run it like this:

```
$ docker run -d \
      --name=k8s \
      -p 8080:8080 \
      gcr.io/google_containers/etcd:3.1.10 \
      etcd --data-dir /var/lib/data
```

Then you will start the API server using a so-called hyperkube *image*, which contains the API server binary. This image is available from the Google Container Registry (GCR) at gcr.io/google_containers/hyperkube:v1.7.11. We use a few settings to serve the API insecurely on a local port. Replace v1.7.11 with the latest version or the one you want to run:

```
$ docker run -d \
      --net=container:k8s \
      gcr.io/google_containers/hyperkube:v1.7.11/ \
      apiserver --etcd-servers=http://127.0.0.1:2379 \
      --service-cluster-ip-range=10.0.0.1/24 \
      --insecure-bind-address=0.0.0.0 \
      --insecure-port=8080 \
      --admission-control=AlwaysAdmit
```

Finally, you can start the admission controller, which points to the API server:

```
$ docker run -d \
      --net=container:k8s \
      gcr.io/google_containers/hyperkube:v1.7.11/ \
      controller-manager --master=127.0.0.1:8080
```

Notice that since etcd, the API server, and the controller-manager share the same network namespace, they can reach each other on 127.0.0.1 even though they are running in different containers.

To test that you have a working setup, use etcdctl in the etcd container and list what is in the */registry* directory:

```
$ docker exec -ti k8s /bin/sh
# export ETCDCTL_API=3
# etcdctl get "/registry/api" --prefix=true
```

You can also reach your Kubernetes API server and start exploring the API:

```
$ curl -s curl http://127.0.0.1:8080/api/v1 | more
{
  "kind": "APIResourceList",
  "groupVersion": "v1",
  "resources": [
    {
      "name": "bindings",
      "singularName": "",
      "namespaced": true,
      "kind": "Binding",
      "verbs": [
        "create"
      ]
    },
  ...
```

So far, you have not started the scheduler, nor have you set up nodes with the kube
let and the kube-proxy. This just shows you how you can run the Kubernetes API
server by starting three local containers.

 It is sometimes helpful to use the hyperkube Docker image to verify some of the configuration options of one of the Kubernetes
binaries. For example, to check the help for the main /apiserver
command, try:

```
$ docker run --rm -ti \
    gcr.io/google_containers/hyperkube:v1.7.11 \
    /apiserver --help
```

Discussion

Though this is a very useful way to start exploring the various Kubernetes components locally, it is not recommended for a production setup.

See Also

- hyperkube Docker images (*https://github.com/kubernetes/kubernetes/tree/master/
  cluster/images/hyperkube*)

2.6 Writing a systemd Unit File to Run Kubernetes Components

Problem

You have used Minikube (see Recipe 1.3) for learning and know how to bootstrap a
Kubernetes cluster using kubeadm (see Recipe 2.2), but you would like to install a

cluster from scratch. To do so, you need to run the Kubernetes components using systemd unit files. You are only looking for a basic examples to run the kubelet via systemd.

Solution

systemd[3] is a system and services manager, sometimes referred to as an init system. It is now the default services manager on Ubuntu 16.04 and CentOS 7.

Checking how kubeadm does it is a very good way to figure out how to do it on your own. If you look closely at the kubeadm configuration, you will see that the kubelet running on every node in your cluster, including the master node, is managed by systemd.

Here is an example, which you can reproduce by logging into any nodes in a cluster built with kubeadm (see Recipe 2.2):

```
# systemctl status kubelet
● kubelet.service - kubelet: The Kubernetes Node Agent
   Loaded: loaded (/lib/systemd/system/kubelet.service; enabled; vendor preset:
           enabled)
  Drop-In: /etc/systemd/system/kubelet.service.d
           └─10-kubeadm.conf
   Active: active (running) since Tue 2017-06-13 08:29:33 UTC; 2 days ago
     Docs: http://kubernetes.io/docs/
 Main PID: 4205 (kubelet)
    Tasks: 17
   Memory: 47.9M
      CPU: 2h 2min 47.666s
   CGroup: /system.slice/kubelet.service
           ├─4205 /usr/bin/kubelet --kubeconfig=/etc/kubernetes/kubelet.conf \
           │                       --require-kubeconfig=true \
           │                       --pod-manifest-path=/etc/kubernetes/manifests \
           │                       --allow-privileged=true \
           │                       --network-plugin=cni \
           │                       --cni-conf
           └─4247 journalctl -k -f
```

This gives you a link to the systemd unit file in */lib/systemd/system/kubelet.service* and its configuration in */etc/systemd/system/kubelet.service.d/10-kubeadm.conf*.

The unit file is straightforward—it points to the kubelet binary installed in */usr/bin*:

```
[Unit]
Description=kubelet: The Kubernetes Node Agent
Documentation=http://kubernetes.io/docs/
```

---

3 freedesktop.org, "systemd" (*https://www.freedesktop.org/wiki/Software/systemd/*).

```
[Service]
ExecStart=/usr/bin/kubelet
Restart=always
StartLimitInterval=0
RestartSec=10

[Install]
WantedBy=multi-user.target
```

The configuration file tells you how the `kubelet` binary is started:

```
[Service]
Environment="KUBELET_KUBECONFIG_ARGS=--kubeconfig=/etc/kubernetes/kubelet.conf
             --require-kubeconfig=true"
Environment="KUBELET_SYSTEM_PODS_ARGS=--pod-manifest-path=/etc/kubernetes/
             manifests --allow-privileged=true"
Environment="KUBELET_NETWORK_ARGS=--network-plugin=cni
             --cni-conf-dir=/etc/cni/net.d --cni-bin-dir=/opt/cni/bin"
Environment="KUBELET_DNS_ARGS=--cluster-dns=10.96.0.10
             --cluster-domain=cluster.local"
Environment="KUBELET_AUTHZ_ARGS=--authorization-mode=Webhook
             --client-ca-file=/etc/kubernetes/pki/ca.crt"
ExecStart=
ExecStart=/usr/bin/kubelet $KUBELET_KUBECONFIG_ARGS $KUBELET_SYSTEM_PODS_ARGS
          $KUBELET_NETWORK_ARGS $KUBELET_DNS_ARGS $KUBELET_AUTHZ_ARGS
          $KUBELET_EXTRA_ARGS
```

All the options specified, such as `--kubeconfig`, defined by the environment variable `$KUBELET_CONFIG_ARGS`, are startup options (*https://kubernetes.io/docs/admin/kube let/*) of the `kubelet` binary.

Discussion

The unit file just shown only deals with the `kubelet`. You can write your own unit files for all the other components of a Kubernetes cluster (i.e., API server, controller-manager, scheduler, proxy). Kubernetes the Hard Way has examples of unit files for each component.[4]

However, you only need to run the `kubelet`. Indeed, the configuration option `--pod-manifest-path` allows you to pass a directory where the `kubelet` will look for manifests that it will automatically start. With `kubeadm`, this directory is used to pass the manifests of the API server, scheduler, `etcd`, and controller-manager. Hence, Kubernetes manages itself and the only thing managed by `systemd` is the `kubelet` process.

---

4 Kubernetes the Hard Way, "Bootstrapping the Kubernetes Control Plane" (*https://github.com/kelseyhightower/kubernetes-the-hard-way/blob/master/docs/08-bootstrapping-kubernetes-controllers.md?*).

To illustrate this, you can list the contents of the */etc/kubernetes/manifests* directory in your kubeadm-based cluster:

```
# ls -l /etc/kubernetes/manifests
total 16
-rw------- 1 root root 1071 Jun 13 08:29 etcd.yaml
-rw------- 1 root root 2086 Jun 13 08:29 kube-apiserver.yaml
-rw------- 1 root root 1437 Jun 13 08:29 kube-controller-manager.yaml
-rw------- 1 root root  857 Jun 13 08:29 kube-scheduler.yaml
```

Looking at the details of the *etcd.yaml* manifest, you can see that it is a Pod with a single container that runs etcd:

```
# cat /etc/kubernetes/manifests/etcd.yaml

apiVersion:        v1
kind:              Pod
metadata:
  creationTimestamp: null
  labels:
    component:     etcd
    tier:          control-plane
  name:            etcd
  namespace:       kube-system
spec:
  containers:
  - command:
    - etcd
    - --listen-client-urls=http://127.0.0.1:2379
    - --advertise-client-urls=http://127.0.0.1:2379
    - --data-dir=/var/lib/etcd
    image:         gcr.io/google_containers/etcd-amd64:3.0.17
  ...
```

See Also

- kubelet configuration options (*https://kubernetes.io/docs/admin/kubelet/*)

2.7 Creating a Kubernetes Cluster on Google Kubernetes Engine (GKE)

Problem

You want to create a Kubernetes cluster on Google Kubernetes Engine (GKE).

Solution

Using the `gcloud` command-line interface, create a Kubernetes cluster with the
`container clusters create` command, like so:

```
$ gcloud container clusters create oreilly
```

By default this will create a Kubernetes cluster with three worker nodes. The master
node is being managed by the GKE service and cannot be accessed.

Discussion

To use GKE, you will first need to do a few things:

- Create an account on the Google Cloud Platform with billing enabled.
- Create a project and enable the GKE service in it.
- Install the `gcloud` CLI on your machine.

To speed up the setup of `gcloud`, you can make use of the Google Cloud Shell (*https://
cloud.google.com/shell/docs/*), a pure online browser-based solution.

Once your cluster is created, you can list it as shown here:

```
$ gcloud container clusters list
NAME     ZONE          MASTER_VERSION  MASTER_IP      ...  STATUS
oreilly  europe-west1-b  1.7.8-gke.0     35.187.80.94   ...  RUNNING
```

> The `gcloud` CLI allows you to resize your cluster, update it, and
> upgrade it:
>
> ```
> ...
> COMMANDS
> ...
>     resize
>         Resizes an existing cluster for running containers.
>     update
>         Update cluster settings for an existing container cluster.
>     upgrade
>         Upgrade the Kubernetes version of an existing container
>         cluster.
> ```

Once you are done using your cluster, do not forget to delete it to avoid being
charged:

```
$ gcloud container clusters delete oreilly
```

See Also

- GKE Quickstart (*https://cloud.google.com/container-engine/docs/quickstart*)
- Google Cloud Shell Quickstart (*https://cloud.google.com/shell/docs/quickstart*)

2.8 Creating a Kubernetes Cluster on Azure Container Service (ACS)

Problem

You want to create a Kubernetes cluster on Azure Container Service (ACS).

Solution

To carry out the following steps, you will need to sign up for a (free) Azure account (*https://azure.microsoft.com/en-us/free/*) and install the Azure CLI (az) version 2.0 (*https://docs.microsoft.com/en-us/cli/azure/install-azure-cli*).

First, make sure that you have the correct az CLI version installed and then log in:

```
$ az --version | grep ^azure-cli
azure-cli (2.0.13)

$ az login
To sign in, use a web browser to open the page https://aka.ms/devicelogin and
enter the code XXXXXXXXX to authenticate.
[
  {
    "cloudName": "AzureCloud",
    "id": "***************************",
    "isDefault": true,
    "name": "Free Trial",
    "state": "Enabled",
    "tenantId": "***************************",
    "user": {
      "name": "******@hotmail.com",
      "type": "user"
    }
  }
]
```

As preparation, create an Azure resource group (the equivalent of a project in Google Cloud) called k8s. This resource group will hold all your resources, such as VMs and networking components, and makes it easy to clean up and tear down later on:

```
$ az group create --name k8s --location northeurope
{
  "id": "/subscriptions/************************/resourceGroups/k8s",
  "location": "northeurope",
  "managedBy": null,
  "name": "k8s",
  "properties": {
    "provisioningState": "Succeeded"
  },
  "tags": null
}
```

 If you're unsure what region (*https://azure.microsoft.com/en-us/ regions/*) to use for the `--location` argument, execute `az account list-locations` and pick one near you.

Now that you have the resource group k8s set up, you can create the cluster with one worker node (*agent* in Azure terminology), like so:

```
$ az acs create --orchestrator-type kubernetes \
                --resource-group k8s \
                --name k8scb \
                --agent-count 1 \
                --generate-ssh-keys
waiting for AAD role to propagate.done
{
...
"provisioningState": "Succeeded",
"template": null,
"templateLink": null,
"timestamp": "2017-08-13T19:02:58.149409+00:00"
},
"resourceGroup": "k8s"
}
```

Note that the `az acs create` command might take up to 10 minutes to complete.

 With the Azure free account you don't have enough quota to create a default (three-agent) Kubernetes cluster, so you will see something like the following if you try it:

```
Operation results in exceeding quota limits of Core.
Maximum allowed: 4, Current in use: 0, Additional
requested: 8.
```

To work around this, either create a smaller cluster (for example, with `--agent-count 1`) or use a paid subscription instead.

As a result, in the Azure portal you should now see something like Figure 2-1. Start by finding the **k8s** resource group and then navigate your way through the Deployments tab.

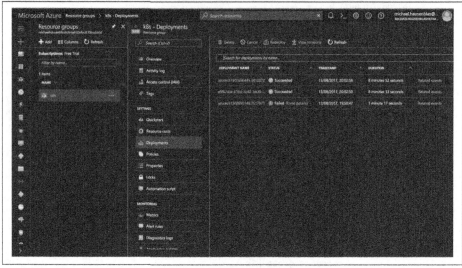

Figure 2-1. Screenshot of the Azure Portal, showing ACS deployments in the k8s resource group

You're now in a position to connect to the cluster:

```
$ az acs kubernetes get-credentials --resource-group=k8s --name=k8scb
```

You can now poke around in the environment and verify the setup:

```
$ kubectl cluster-info
Kubernetes master is running at https://k8scb-k8s-143f1emgmt.northeurope.cloudapp
  .azure.com
Heapster is running at https://k8scb-k8s-143f1emgmt.northeurope.cloudapp.azure
  .com/api/v1/namespaces/kube-system/services/heapster/proxy
KubeDNS is running at https://k8scb-k8s-143f1emgmt.northeurope.cloudapp.azure
  .com/api/v1/namespaces/kube-system/services/kube-dns/proxy
kubernetes-dashboard is running at https://k8scb-k8s-143f1emgmt.northeurope
  .cloudapp.azure.com/api/v1/namespaces/kube-system/services/kubernetes-dashboard
  /proxy
tiller-deploy is running at https://k8scb-k8s-143f1emgmt.northeurope.cloudapp
  .azure.com/api/v1/namespaces/kube-system/services/tiller-deploy/proxy

To further debug and diagnose cluster problems, use 'kubectl cluster-info dump'.

$ kubectl get nodes
NAME                      STATUS                   AGE    VERSION
k8s-agent-1a7972f2-0      Ready                    7m     v1.7.8
k8s-master-1a7972f2-0     Ready,SchedulingDisabled 7m     v1.7.8
```

And indeed, as you can see from the output that there is one agent (worker) node and one master node.

When you're done discovering ACS, don't forget to shut down the cluster and remove all the resources by deleting the resource group k8s:

```
$ az group delete --name k8s --yes --no-wait
```

Although the `az group delete` command returns immediately, it can take up to 10 minutes for all the resources—such as VMs, virtual networks, or disks—to be removed and the resource group actually destroyed. You might want to check in the Azure portal to make sure everything went according to plan.

 If you don't want to or cannot install the Azure CLI, you can use the Azure Cloud Shell (*https://azure.microsoft.com/en-us/features/cloud-shell/*) from within your browser instead to carry out the preceding steps to install the Kubernetes cluster.

See Also

- "Deploy Kubernetes cluster for Linux containers" (*https://docs.microsoft.com/en-us/azure/container-service/kubernetes/container-service-kubernetes-walkthrough*) in the Microsoft Azure documentation

## CHAPTER 3

Learning to Use the Kubernetes Client

This chapter gathers recipes around the basic usage of the Kubernetes command-line interface (CLI), kubectl. See Chapter 1 for how to install the CLI tool; for advanced use cases, see Chapter 6, where we show how to use the Kubernetes API.

3.1 Listing Resources

Problem

You want to list Kubernetes resources of a certain kind.

Solution

Use the get verb of kubectl along with the resource type. To list all pods:

```
$ kubectl get pods
```

To list all services and deployments:

```
$ kubectl get services,deployments
```

To list a specific deployment:

```
$ kubectl get deployment myfirstk8sapp
```

To list all resources:

```
$ kubectl get all
```

Note that kubectl get is a very basic but extremely useful command to get a quick overview what is going on in the cluster—it's essentially the equivalent to ps on Unix.

Many resources have short names you can use with kubectl, spar-
ing your time and sanity. Here are some examples:

- configmaps (aka cm)
- daemonsets (aka ds)
- deployments (aka deploy)
- endpoints (aka ep)
- events (aka ev)
- horizontalpodautoscalers (aka hpa)
- ingresses (aka ing)
- namespaces (aka ns)
- nodes (aka no)
- persistentvolumeclaims (aka pvc)
- persistentvolumes (aka pv)
- pods (aka po)
- replicasets (aka rs)
- replicationcontrollers (aka rc)
- resourcequotas (aka quota)
- serviceaccounts (aka sa)
- services (aka svc)

3.2 Deleting Resources

Problem

You no longer need resources and want to get rid of them.

Solution

Use the delete verb of kubectl along with the type and name of the resource you
wish to delete.

To delete all resources in the namespace my-app, do:

```
$ kubectl get ns
NAME          STATUS   AGE
default       Active   2d
kube-public   Active   2d
kube-system   Active   2d
```

```
my-app        Active    20m
```
```
$ kubectl delete ns my-app
namespace "my-app" deleted
```

If you're wondering how to create a namespace, see Recipe 6.3.

You can also delete specific resources and/or influence the process by which they are destroyed. To delete services and deployments labeled with app=niceone, do:

```
$ kubectl delete svc,deploy -l app=niceone
```

To force deletion of a pod, do:

```
$ kubectl delete pod hangingpod --grace-period=0 --force
```

To delete all pods in the namespace test, do:

```
$ kubectl delete pods --all --namespace test
```

Discussion

Do not delete supervised objects such as pods controlled by a deployment directly. Rather, kill their supervisors or use dedicated operations to get rid of the managed resources. For example, if you scale a deployment to zero replicas (see Recipe 9.1), then you effectively delete all the pods it looks after.

Another aspect to take into account is cascading versus direct deletion—for example, when you delete a custom resource definition (CRD) as shown in Recipe 13.4, all its dependent objects are deleted too. To learn more about how to influence the cascading deletion policy, read Garbage Collection (*https://kubernetes.io/docs/concepts/work loads/controllers/garbage-collection/*) in the Kubernetes docs.

3.3 Watching Resource Changes with kubectl

Problem

You want to watch the changes to Kubernetes objects in an interactive manner in the terminal.

Solution

The kubectl command has a --watch option that gives you this behavior. For example, to watch pods:

```
$ kubectl get pods --watch
```

Note that this is a blocking and autoupdating command, akin to top.

Discussion

The --watch option is useful, but sometimes not very reliable, in terms of refreshing the screen correctly. Alternatively, you can use the watch (*http://man7.org/linux/man-pages/man1/watch.1.html*) command, as in:

```
$ watch kubectl get pods
```

3.4 Editing Resources with kubectl

Problem

You want to update the property of a Kubernetes resource.

Solution

Use the edit verb of kubectl along with the resource type:

```
$ kubectl run nginx --image=nginx
$ kubectl edit deploy/nginx
```

Now edit the nginx deployment in your editor—for example, change replicas to 2. Once you save, you'll see something like:

```
deployment "nginx" edited
```

Discussion

If you have editor issues, use EDITOR=vi. Also be aware that not all changes trigger a deployment.

Some triggers have shortcuts, for example, if you want to change the image version a deployment uses, simply use kubectl set image, which updates the existing container images of resources (valid for deployments, replica sets/replication controllers, daemon sets, jobs, and simple pods).

3.5 Asking kubectl to Explain Resources and Fields

Problem

You want to gain a deeper understanding of a certain resource—for example, service —and/or understand what exactly a certain field in a Kubernetes manifest means, including default values and if it's required or optional.

Solution

Use the explain verb of kubectl:

```
$ kubectl explain svc
DESCRIPTION:
Service is a named abstraction of software service (for example, mysql)
consisting of local port (for example 3306) that the proxy listens on, and the
selector that determines which pods will answer requests sent through the proxy.

FIELDS:
   status       <Object>
     Most recently observed status of the service. Populated by the system.
     Read-only. More info: https://git.k8s.io/community/contributors/devel/
     api-conventions.md#spec-and-status/

   apiVersion    <string>
     APIVersion defines the versioned schema of this representation of an
     object. Servers should convert recognized schemas to the latest internal
     value, and may reject unrecognized values. More info:
     https://git.k8s.io/community/contributors/devel/api-conventions.md#resources

   kind <string>
     Kind is a string value representing the REST resource this object
     represents. Servers may infer this from the endpoint the client submits
     requests to. Cannot be updated. In CamelCase. More info:
     https://git.k8s.io/community/contributors/devel/api-conventions
     .md#types-kinds

   metadata      <Object>
     Standard object's metadata. More info:
     https://git.k8s.io/community/contributors/devel/api-conventions.md#metadata

   spec <Object>
     Spec defines the behavior of a service. https://git.k8s.io/community/
     contributors/devel/api-conventions.md#spec-and-status/
```

```
$ kubectl explain svc.spec.externalIPs
FIELD: externalIPs <[]string>

DESCRIPTION:
     externalIPs is a list of IP addresses for which nodes in the cluster will
     also accept traffic for this service.  These IPs are not managed by
     Kubernetes.  The user is responsible for ensuring that traffic arrives at a
     node with this IP.  A common example is external load-balancers that are not
     part of the Kubernetes system.
```

Discussion

The `kubectl explain` command[1] pulls the descriptions of resources and fields from the Swagger/OpenAPI definitions,[2] exposed by the API server.

See Also

- Ross Kukulinski's blog post, "kubectl explain—#HeptioProTip" (*https://blog.heptio.com/kubectl-explain-heptioprotip-ee883992a243*)

---

1 Kubernetes, "Kubectl Reference Docs: Explain" (*https://kubernetes.io/docs/reference/generated/kubectl/kubectl-commands#explain*).

2 Kubernetes, "The Kubernetes API" (*https://kubernetes.io/docs/concepts/overview/kubernetes-api/*).

## CHAPTER 4

Creating and Modifying Fundamental Workloads

In this chapter, we present recipes that show you how to manage fundamental Kubernetes workload types: pods and deployments. We show how to create deployments and pods via CLI commands and from a YAML manifest, and explain how to scale and update a deployment.

4.1 Creating a Deployment Using kubectl run

Problem

You want to quickly launch a long-running application such as a web server.

Solution

Use the kubectl run command, a generator that creates a deployment manifest on the fly. For example, to create a deployment that runs the Ghost microblogging platform do the following:

```
$ kubectl run ghost --image=ghost:0.9

$ kubectl get deploy/ghost
NAME      DESIRED   CURRENT   UP-TO-DATE   AVAILABLE   AGE
ghost     1         1         1            0           16s
```

Discussion

The `kubectl run` command can take a number of arguments to configure additional parameters of the deployments. For example, you can do the following:

- Set environment variables with `--env`
- Define container ports with `--port`
- Define a command to run using `--command`
- Automatically create an associated service with `--expose`
- Define the number of pods using `--replicas`

Typical usages are as follows. To launch Ghost serving on port 2368 and create a service along with it, enter:

```
$ kubectl run ghost --image=ghost:0.9 --port=2368 --expose
```

To launch MySQL with the root password set, enter:

```
$ kubectl run mysql --image=mysql:5.5 --env=MYSQL_ROOT_PASSWORD=root
```

To launch a busybox container and execute the command `sleep 3600` on start, enter:

```
$ kubectl run myshell --image=busybox --command -- sh -c "sleep 3600"
```

See also `kubectl run --help` for more details about the available arguments.

4.2 Creating Objects from File Manifests

Problem

Rather than creating an object via a generator such as `kubectl run`, you want to explicitly state its properties and then create it.

Solution

Use `kubectl create` like so:

```
$ kubectl create -f <manifest>
```

In Recipe 6.3 you'll see how to create a namespace using a YAML manifest. This is one of the simplest examples as the manifest is very short. It can be written in YAML or JSON—for example, with a YAML manifest file *myns.yaml* like so:

```
apiVersion:    v1
kind:          namespace
metadata:
  name:        myns
```

You can create this object with kubectl create -f myns.yaml.

Discussion

You can point kubectl create to a URL instead, or a filename in your local filesystem. For example, to create the frontend for the canonical Guestbook application, get the URL of the raw YAML that defines the application in a single manifest and enter:

```
$ kubectl create -f https://raw.githubusercontent.com/kubernetes/kubernetes/ \
               master/examples/guestbook/frontend-deployment.yaml
```

4.3 Writing a Pod Manifest from Scratch

Problem

You want to write a pod manifest from scratch and not use a generator such as kubectl run.

Solution

A Pod is an /api/v1 object and, like any other Kubernetes object, its manifest file contains the following fields:

- apiVersion, which specifies the API version
- kind, which indicates the type of the object
- metadata, which provides some metadata about the object
- spec, which provides the object specification

The pod manifest contains an array of containers and an optional array of volumes (see Chapter 8). In its simplest form, with a single container and no volume, it looks as follows:

```
apiVersion:   v1
kind:         Pod
metadata:
  name:       oreilly
spec:
  containers:
  - name:     oreilly
    image:    nginx
```

Save this YAML manifest in a file called *oreilly.yaml* and then use kubectl to create it:

```
$ kubectl create -f oreilly.yaml
```

Discussion

The API specification of a pod is much richer than what is shown in the Solution, which is the most basic functioning pod. For example, a pod can contain multiple containers, as shown here:

```
apiVersion: v1
kind:       Pod
metadata:
  name:     oreilly
spec:
  containers:
  - name:   oreilly
    image:  nginx
  - name:   safari
    image:  redis
```

A pod can also contain volume definitions to load data in the containers (see Recipe 8.1), as well as probes to check the health of the containerized application (see Recipe 11.2 and Recipe 11.3).

A description of the thinking behind many of the specification fields and a link to the full API object specification is detailed in the documentation (*https://kubernetes.io/docs/concepts/workloads/pods/pod/*).

 Unless for very specific reasons, never create a pod on its own. Use a Deployment object (see Recipe 4.4) to supervise pods—it will watch over the pods through another object called a ReplicaSet.

See Also

- Kubernetes Pods reference documentation (*https://kubernetes.io/docs/api-reference/v1.7/#pod-v1-core*).

- ReplicaSet documentation (*https://kubernetes.io/docs/concepts/workloads/control lers/replicaset/*)

4.4 Launching a Deployment Using a Manifest

Problem

You want to have full control over how a (long-running) app is launched and supervised.

Solution

Write a manifest using the `Deployment` object in it. For the basics, see also Recipe 4.3.

Let's say you have manifest file called *fancyapp.yaml* with the following content:

```
apiVersion:      extensions/v1beta1
kind:            Deployment
metadata:
  name:          fancyapp
spec:
  replicas:      5
  template:
    metadata:
      labels:
        app:     fancy
        env:     development
    spec:
      containers:
      - name:    sise
        image:   mhausenblas/simpleservice:0.5.0
        ports:
        - containerPort: 9876
        env:
        - name:  SIMPLE_SERVICE_VERSION
          value: "0.9"
```

As you can see, there are a couple of things you might want to do explicitly when launching the app:

- Set the number of pods (`replicas`), or identical copies, that should be launched and supervised.

- Label it, such as with `env=development` (see also Recipe 6.5 and Recipe 6.6).

- Set environment variables, such as `SIMPLE_SERVICE_VERSION`.

Now let's have a look at what the deployment entails:

```
$ kubectl create -f fancyapp.yaml
deployment "fancyapp" created

$ kubectl get deploy
NAME        DESIRED   CURRENT   UP-TO-DATE   AVAILABLE   AGE
fancyapp    5         5         5            0           8s

$ kubectl get rs
NAME                  DESIRED   CURRENT   READY   AGE
fancyapp-1223770997   5         5         0       13s

$ kubectl get po
NAME                        READY   STATUS             RESTARTS   AGE
fancyapp-1223770997-18msl   0/1     ContainerCreating  0          15s
```

```
fancyapp-1223770997-1zdg4    0/1    ContainerCreating    0    15s
fancyapp-1223770997-6rqn2    0/1    ContainerCreating    0    15s
fancyapp-1223770997-7bnbh    0/1    ContainerCreating    0    15s
fancyapp-1223770997-qxg4v    0/1    ContainerCreating    0    15s
```

And if we repeat this a few seconds later:

```
$ kubectl get po
NAME                         READY   STATUS    RESTARTS   AGE
fancyapp-1223770997-18msl    1/1     Running   0          1m
fancyapp-1223770997-1zdg4    1/1     Running   0          1m
fancyapp-1223770997-6rqn2    1/1     Running   0          1m
fancyapp-1223770997-7bnbh    1/1     Running   0          1m
fancyapp-1223770997-qxg4v    1/1     Running   0          1m
```

 When you want to get rid of a deployment, and with it the replica sets and pods it supervises, execute a command like kubectl delete deploy/fancyapp. Do *not* try to delete individual pods, as they will be recreated by the deployment. This is something that often confuses beginners.

Deployments allow you to scale the app (see Recipe 9.1) as well as roll out a new version or roll back to a previous version. They are, in general, good for stateless apps that require pods with identical characteristics.

Discussion

A deployment is a supervisor for pods and replica sets (RSs), giving you fine-grained control over how and when a new pod version is rolled out or rolled back to a previous state. The RSs and pods that a deployment supervises are generally of no interest to you unless, for example, you need to debug a pod (see Recipe 12.5). Figure 4-1 illustrates how you can move back and forth between deployment revisions.

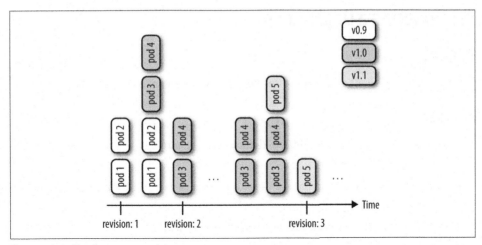

Figure 4-1. Deployment revisions

Note that RS will, going forward, replace the original replication controller (RC), so it's a good thing to start thinking in terms of RSs rather than RCs. For now, the only difference is that RSs support set-based labels/querying, but we can expect that there will be more features added to the RS and the RC will eventually be deprecated.

Finally, to generate the manifest, you can use the `kubectl create` command and the `--dry-run` option. It will allow you to generate the manifest in YAML or JSON format and save the manifest for later use. For example, to create the manifest of a deployment called `fancy-app` using the Docker image `nginx`, issue the following command:

```
$ kubectl create deployment fancyapp --image nginx -o json --dry-run
{
    "kind": "Deployment",
    "apiVersion": "extensions/v1beta1",
    "metadata": {
        "name": "fancy-app",
        "creationTimestamp": null,
        "labels": {
            "app": "fancy-app"
        }
    },
...
```

See Also

- Kubernetes Deployments in documentation (*https://kubernetes.io/docs/concepts/workloads/controllers/deployment/*)

4.5 Updating a Deployment

Problem

You have a deployment and want to roll out a new version of your app.

Solution

Update your deployment and let the default update strategy, RollingUpdate, automatically handle the rollout.

For example, suppose you create a new container image and want to update the deployment based on it:

```
$ kubectl run sise --image=mhausenblas/simpleservice:0.4.0
deployment "sise" created

$ kubectl set image deployment sise mhausenblas/simpleservice:0.5.0
deployment "sise" image updated

$ kubectl rollout status deployment sise
deployment "sise" successfully rolled out

$ kubectl rollout history deployment sise
deployments "sise"
REVISION        CHANGE-CAUSE
1               <none>
2               <none>
```

You've now successfully rolled out a new revision of your deployment where only the container image used has changed. All other properties of the deployment, such as the number of replicas, stay unchanged. But what if you want to update other aspects of the deployment, such as changing environment variables? You can use a number of kubectl commands to update the deployment. For example, to add a port definition to the current deployment, you can use kubectl edit:

```
$ kubectl edit deploy sise
```

This command will open the current deployment in your default editor, or, when set and exported, in the editor specified by the environment variable KUBE_EDITOR.

Say you want to add the following port definition:

```
...
  ports:
  - containerPort: 9876
...
```

The result of the editing process (in this case, with KUBE_EDITOR set to vi) is shown in Figure 4-2.

```
 1 # Please edit the object below. Lines beginning with a '#' will be ignored,
 2 # and an empty file will abort the edit. If an error occurs while saving this file will be
 3 # reopened with the relevant failures.
 4 #
 5 apiVersion: extensions/v1beta1
 6 kind: Deployment
 7 metadata:
 8   annotations:
 9     deployment.kubernetes.io/revision: "2"
10   creationTimestamp: 2017-10-18T09:32:01Z
11   generation: 2
12   labels:
13     run: sise
14   name: sise
15   namespace: default
16   resourceVersion: "762856"
17   selfLink: /apis/extensions/v1beta1/namespaces/default/deployments/sise
18   uid: 322b6e48-b3e7-11e7-ad6d-080027390640
19 spec:
20   replicas: 1
21   selector:
22     matchLabels:
23       run: sise
24   strategy:
25     rollingUpdate:
26       maxSurge: 1
27       maxUnavailable: 1
28     type: RollingUpdate
29   template:
30     metadata:
31       creationTimestamp: null
32       labels:
33         run: sise
34     spec:
35       containers:
36       - image: mhausenblas/simpleservice:0.5.0
37         imagePullPolicy: IfNotPresent
38         name: sise
39         ports:
40         - containerPort: 9876
41         resources: {}
42         terminationMessagePath: /dev/termination-log
43         terminationMessagePolicy: File
44       dnsPolicy: ClusterFirst
45       restartPolicy: Always
46       schedulerName: default-scheduler
47       securityContext: {}
48       terminationGracePeriodSeconds: 30
49 status:
50   availableReplicas: 1
-- INSERT --
```

Figure 4-2. Editing a deployment

Once you save and exit the editor, Kubernetes kicks off a new deployment, now with the port defined. Let's verify that:

```
$ kubectl rollout history deployment sise
deployments "sise"
REVISION        CHANGE-CAUSE
1               <none>
2               <none>
3               <none>
```

Indeed, we see that revision 3 has been rolled out with the changes we introduced with kubectl edit. The reason the CHANGE-CAUSE column is empty is that you didn't use kubectl create with the --record option. If you want to see what triggered a revision, add this option.

As mentioned earlier, there are more kubectl commands that you can use to update your deployment:

- Use kubectl apply to update a deployment (or create it if it doesn't exist) from a manifest file—for example, kubectl apply -f simpleservice.yaml.

- Use kubectl replace to replace a deployment from a manifest file—for example, kubectl replace -f simpleservice.yaml. Note that unlike apply, in order to use replace, the deployment must already exist.

- Use kubectl patch to update a specific key—for example:

```
kubectl patch deployment sise -p '{"spec": {"template":
{"spec": {"containers":
[{"name": "sise", "image": "mhausenblas/simpleservice:0.5.0"}]}}}}'
```

What if you make a mistake or experience issues with the new version of the deployment? Luckily, Kubernetes makes it really easy to roll back to a known good state using the kubectl rollout undo command. For example, suppose the last edit was a mistake and you want to roll back to revision 2. You can do this with the following command:

```
$ kubectl rollout undo deployment sise —to-revision=2
```

You can then verify that the port definition has been removed with kubectl get deploy/sise -o yaml.

 The rollout of a deployment is only triggered if parts of the pod template (that is, keys below .spec.template) are changed, such as environment variables, ports, or the container image. Changes to aspects of the deployments, such as the replica count, do not trigger a new deployment.

## CHAPTER 5

Working with Services

In this chapter, we discuss how pods communicate within the cluster, how applications discover each other, and how to expose pods so that they can be accessed from outside of the cluster.

The primitive we will be using here is called a Kubernetes *service* (*https://kubernetes.io/docs/concepts/services-networking/service/*), as depicted in Figure 5-1.

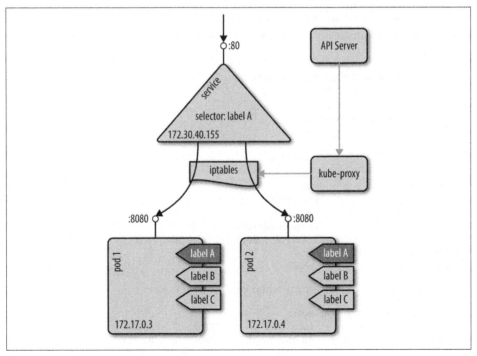

Figure 5-1. The Kubernetes service concept

A service provides a stable virtual IP (VIP) address (*https://blog.openshift.com/ kubernetes-services-by-example/*) for a set of pods. Though pods may come and go, services allow clients to reliably discover and connect to the containers running in the pods by using the VIP. The "virtual" in VIP means it's not an actual IP address connected to a network interface; its purpose is purely to forward traffic to one or more pods. Keeping the mapping between the VIP and the pods up to date is the job of kube-proxy, a process that runs on every node on the cluster. This kube-proxy process queries the API server to learn about new services in the cluster and updates the node's iptables rules (iptables) accordingly, to provide the necessary routing information.

5.1 Creating a Service to Expose Your Application

Problem

You want to provide a stable and reliable way to discover and access your application within the cluster.

Solution

Create a Kubernetes service for the pods that make up your application.

Assuming you created an nginx deployment with kubectl run nginx --image nginx, you can automatically create a Service object using the kubectl expose command, like so:

```
$ kubectl expose deploy/nginx --port 80
service "nginx" exposed

$ kubectl describe svc/nginx
Name:                nginx
Namespace:           default
Labels:              run=nginx
Annotations:         <none>
Selector:            run=nginx
Type:                ClusterIP
IP:                  10.0.0.143
Port:                <unset> 80/TCP
Endpoints:           172.17.0.5:80,172.17.0.7:80
Session Affinity:    None
Events:              <none>
```

You will then see the object appear when you list all services:

```
$ kubectl get svc | grep nginx
NAME       TYPE        CLUSTER-IP     EXTERNAL-IP   PORT(S)   AGE
nginx      ClusterIP   10.109.24.56   <none>        80/TCP    2s
```

Discussion

To access this service via your browser, run a proxy in a separate terminal, like so:

```
$ kubectl proxy
Starting to serve on 127.0.0.1:8001
```

Then open your browser with:

```
$ open http://localhost:8001/api/v1/proxy/namespaces/default/services/nginx/
```

If you wanted to write a Service object by hand for the same nginx deployment, you would write the following YAML file:

```
apiVersion:  v1
kind:        Service
metadata:
  name:      nginx
spec:
  selector:
    run:     nginx
  ports:
  - port:    80
```

The one thing to pay attention to in this YAML file is the *selector,* which is used to select all the pods that make up this microservice abstraction. Kubernetes uses the Service object to dynamically configure the iptables on all the nodes to be able to send the network traffic to the containers that make up the microservice. The selection is done as a label query (see Recipe 6.6) and results in a list of endpoints.

 If your service does not seem to be working properly, check the labels used in the selector and verify that a set of endpoints is being populated with kubectl get endpoints. If not, this most likely means that your selector is not finding any matching pods.

 Pod supervisors, such as deployments or replication controllers, operate orthogonally to services. Both supervisors and services find the pods they're looking after by using labels, but they have different jobs to do: supervisors monitor the health of and restart pods, and services make them accessible in a reliable way.

See Also

- Kubernetes Services documentation (*https://kubernetes.io/docs/concepts/services-networking/service*)

- Kubernetes tutorial "Using a Service to Expose Your App" (*https://kubernetes.io/docs/tutorials/kubernetes-basics/expose-intro/*)

5.2 Verifying the DNS Entry of a Service

Problem

You have created a service (see Recipe 5.1) and want to verify that your DNS registration is working properly.

Solution

By default Kubernetes uses `ClusterIP` as the service type, and that exposes the service on a cluster-internal IP. If the DNS cluster add-on is available and working properly, you can access the service via a fully qualified domain name (FQDN) in the form of `$SERVICENAME.$NAMESPACE.svc.cluster.local`.

To verify that this is working as expected, get an interactive shell within a container in your cluster. The easiest way to do this is to use `kubectl run` with the busybox image, like so:

```
$ kubectl run busybox --image busybox -it -- /bin/sh
If you don't see a command prompt, try pressing enter.

/ # nslookup nginx
Server:    10.96.0.10
Address 1: 10.96.0.10 kube-dns.kube-system.svc.cluster.local

Name:      nginx
Address 1: 10.109.24.56 nginx.default.svc.cluster.local
```

The IP address returned for the service should correspond to its cluster IP.

5.3 Changing the Type of a Service

Problem

You have an existing service, say of type `ClusterIP`, as discussed in Recipe 5.2 and you want to change its type so that you can expose your application as a `NodePort` or via a cloud provider load balancer using the `LoadBalancer` service type.

Solution

Use the `kubectl edit` command along with your preferred editor to change the service type. Suppose you have a manifest file called *simple-nginx-svc.yaml* with this content:

```
kind:      Service
apiVersion: v1
metadata:
  name:      webserver
spec:
  ports:
  - port:    80
  selector:
    app:     nginx
```

Create the webserver service and query for it:

```
$ kubectl create -f simple-nginx-svc.yaml
```

```
$ kubectl get svc/webserver
NAME        CLUSTER-IP    EXTERNAL-IP    PORT(S)    AGE
webserver   10.0.0.39     <none>         80/TCP     56s
```

Next, change the service type to, say, NodePort, like so:

```
$ kubectl edit svc/webserver
```

This command will download the current spec the API server has of the service and open it in your default editor, resulting in something like what's shown in Figure 5-2 (EDITOR=vi is set here).

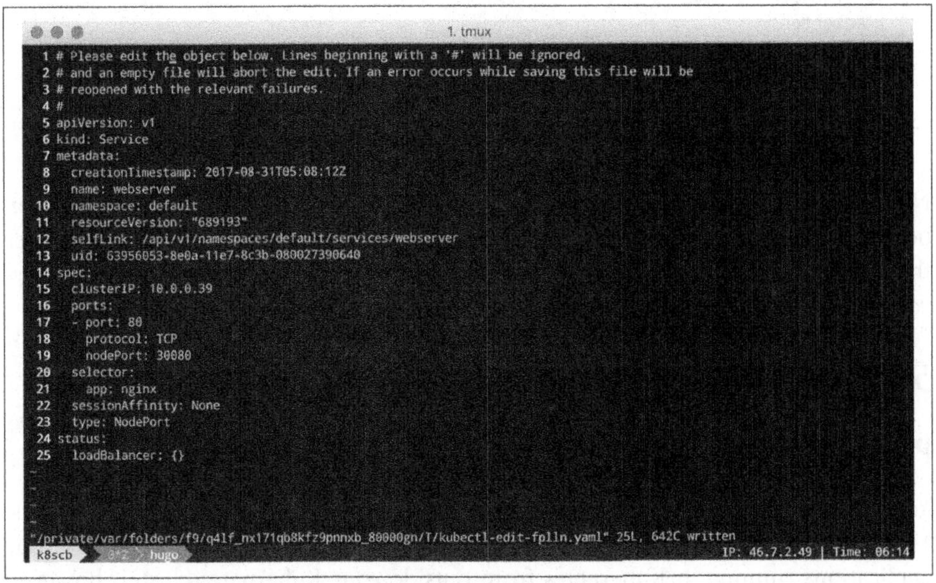

Figure 5-2. Screenshot of editing service using kubectl edit

Once you've saved the edits (changing `type` to `NodePort` and `containerPort` to `node Port`), you can verify the updated service, like so:

```
$ kubectl get svc/webserver
NAME        CLUSTER-IP   EXTERNAL-IP   PORT(S)       AGE
webserver   10.0.0.39    <nodes>       80:30080/TCP  7m

$ kubectl get svc/webserver -o yaml
apiVersion: v1
kind: Service
metadata:
  creationTimestamp: 2017-08-31T05:08:12Z
  name: webserver
  namespace: default
  resourceVersion: "689727"
  selfLink: /api/v1/namespaces/default/services/webserver
  uid: 63956053-8e0a-11e7-8c3b-080027390640
spec:
  clusterIP: 10.0.0.39
  externalTrafficPolicy: Cluster
  ports:
  - nodePort: 30080
    port: 80
    protocol: TCP
    targetPort: 80
  selector:
    app: nginx
  sessionAffinity: None
  type: NodePort
status:
  loadBalancer: {}
```

Note that you can change the service type to whatever suits your use case; however, be aware of the implications of certain types, like `LoadBalancer`, which may trigger the provisioning of public cloud infrastructure components that can be costly if used without awareness and/or monitoring.

5.4 Deploying an Ingress Controller on Minikube

Problem

You want to deploy an ingress controller on Minikube to learn about `Ingress` objects. `Ingress` objects are of interest to you because you want to provide access to your applications running in Kubernetes from outside your Kubernetes cluster; however, you do not want to create a `NodePort`- or `LoadBalancer`-type service.

Solution

For `Ingress` objects (discussed in Recipe 5.5) to take effect and provide a route from outside the cluster to your pods, you need to deploy an ingress controller.

On Minikube, enable the ingress add-on like so:

```
$ minikube addons enable ingress
```

Once done, you should see ingress appear as enabled in the list of Minikube add-ons. Check that this is the case with:

```
$ minikube addons list | grep ingress
- ingress: enabled
```

After a minute or less, two new pods will start in your `kube-system` namespace:

```
$ kubectl get pods -n kube-system
NAME                           READY   STATUS    RESTARTS   AGE
default-http-backend-6tv69     1/1     Running   1          1d
...
nginx-ingress-controller-95dqr 1/1     Running   1          1d
...
```

You are now ready to create `Ingress` objects.

See Also

- Ingress documentation (*https://kubernetes.io/docs/concepts/services-networking/ingress/*)
- Nginx-based ingress controller (*https://github.com/kubernetes/ingress-nginx/blob/master/README.md*)

5.5 Making Services Accessible from Outside the Cluster

Problem

You want to access a Kubernetes service from outside of the cluster.

Solution

Use an ingress controller (see Recipe 5.4), which is configured by creating `Ingress` objects. The following shows the manifest of an `Ingress` rule that configures a path to an nginx service:

```
$ cat nginx-ingress.yaml
kind:                          Ingress
apiVersion:                    extensions/v1beta1
```

```
metadata:
  name:                          nginx-public
  annotations:
    ingress.kubernetes.io/rewrite-target: /
spec:
  rules:
  - host:
    http:
      paths:
        - path:                  /web
          backend:
            serviceName:         nginx
            servicePort:         80
```

```
$ kubectl create -f nginx-ingress.yaml
```

Now you can see the `Ingress` object created for nginx in your Kubernetes dashboard (Figure 5-3).

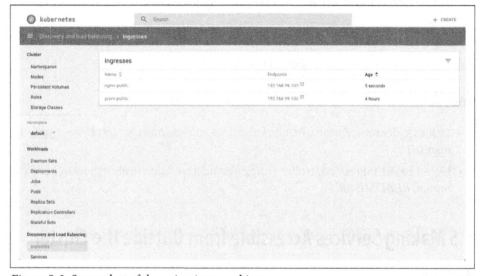

Figure 5-3. Screenshot of the nginx ingress object

From the Kubernetes dashboard, you can see that nginx will be available via the IP address 192.168.99.100, and the manifest file defines that it should be exposed via the path /web. Based on this information, you can access nginx from outside the cluster now as follows:

```
$ curl -k https://192.168.99.100/web
<!DOCTYPE html>
<html>
<head>
<title>Welcome to nginx!</title>
<style>
```

```
    body {
        width: 35em;
        margin: 0 auto;
        font-family: Tahoma, Verdana, Arial, sans-serif;
    }
</style>
</head>
<body>
<h1>Welcome to nginx!</h1>
<p>If you see this page, the nginx web server is successfully installed and
working. Further configuration is required.</p>

<p>For online documentation and support please refer to
<a href="http://nginx.org/">nginx.org</a>.<br/>
Commercial support is available at
<a href="http://nginx.com/">nginx.com</a>.</p>

<p><em>Thank you for using nginx.</em></p>
</body>
</html>
```

Discussion

In general, ingress works as depicted in Figure 5-4: the ingress controller listens to the /ingresses endpoint of the API server, learning about new rules. It then configures the routes so that external traffic lands at a specific (cluster-internal) service—service1 on port 9876 in our example.

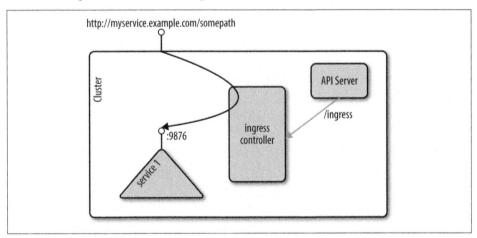

Figure 5-4. Ingress concept

This recipe uses Minishift, where an ingress controller add-on is readily available. Usually, you'll need to set up an ingress controller yourself; see for example the instructions on GitHub (*https://github.com/kubernetes/ingress-nginx*).

See Also

- The kubernetes/ingress-nginx repo on GitHub (*https://github.com/kubernetes/ingress*)
- Milos Gajdos's blog post "Kubernetes Services and Ingress Under X-ray" (*http://containerops.org/2017/01/30/kubernetes-services-and-ingress-under-x-ray/*)
- Daemonza's blog post "Kubernetes nginx-ingress-controller" (*https://daemonza.github.io/2017/02/13/kubernetes-nginx-ingress-controller/*)

## CHAPTER 6

Exploring the Kubernetes API and Key Metadata

In this chapter, we present recipes that address the basic interaction with Kubernetes objects as well as the API. Every object in Kubernetes, no matter if namespaced like a deployment or cluster-wide like a node, has certain fields available—for example, `metadata`, `spec`, and `status`.[1] The `spec` describes the desired state for an object (the specification), and the `status` captures the actual state of the object, managed by the Kubernetes API server.

6.1 Discovering API Endpoints of the Kubernetes API Server

Problem

You want to discover the various API endpoints available on the Kubernetes API server.

Solution

If you have access to the API server via an unauthenticated private port, you can directly issue HTTP requests to the API server and explore the various endpoints. For example, with Minikube, you can `ssh` inside the virtual machine (`minikube ssh`) and reach the API server on port 8080, as shown here:

---

1 Kubernetes, "Understanding Kubernetes Objects" (*https://kubernetes.io/docs/concepts/overview/working-with-objects/kubernetes-objects/*).

```
$ curl localhost:8080/api/v1
...
{
    "name": "pods",
    "namespaced": true,
    "kind": "Pod",
    "verbs": [
      "create",
      "delete",
      "deletecollection",
      "get",
      "list",
      "patch",
      "proxy",
      "update",
      "watch"
    ],
    "shortNames": [
      "po"
    ]
  },
...
```

In this listing you see an example of an object of kind Pod as well as the allowed operations on this subject, such as get and delete.

 Alternatively, if you don't have direct access to the machine the Kubernetes API server is running on, you can use kubectl to proxy the API locally. This will allow you to reach the API server locally, but using an authenticated session:

```
$ kubectl proxy --port=8001 --api-prefix=/
```

And then in another window, do this:

```
$ curl localhost:8001/foobar
```

The use of the /foobar API path allows you to list all the API endpoints. Note that both --port and --api-prefix are optional.

Discussion

When discovering the API endpoints, you will see different ones, like:

- /api/v1
- /apis/apps
- /apis/authentication.k8s.io
- /apis/authorization.k8s.io
- /apis/autoscaling

- /apis/batch

Each of these endpoints corresponds to an API group. Within a group, API objects are versioned (e.g., v1beta1, v1beta2) to indicate the maturity of the objects. Pods, services, config maps, and secrets, for example, are all part of the /api/v1 API group, whereas deployments are part of the /apis/extensions/v1beta1 API group.

The group an object is part of is what is referred to as the apiVersion in the object specification, available via the API reference (*https://kubernetes.io/docs/api-reference/v1.7/*).

See Also

- Kubernetes API Overview (*https://kubernetes.io/docs/reference/api-overview/*)
- Kubernetes API Conventions (*https://github.com/kubernetes/community/blob/master/contributors/devel/api-conventions.md*)

6.2 Understanding the Structure of a Kubernetes Manifest

Problem

While Kubernetes has a few convenience generators with kubectl run and kubectl create, you need to learn how to write Kubernetes manifests, expressing Kubernetes object specifications. To do this, you need to understand the general structure of manifests.

Solution

In Recipe 6.1, you learned about the various API groups and how to discover which group a particular object is in.

All API resources are either objects or lists. All resources have a kind and an apiVersion. In addition, every object kind must have metadata. The metadata contains the name of the object, the namespace it is in (see Recipe 6.3), and potentially some labels (see Recipe 6.6) and annotations (see Recipe 6.7).

A pod, for example, will be of kind Pod and apiVersion v1, and the beginning of a simple manifest written in YAML will look like this:

```
apiVersion: v1
kind: Pod
metadata:
  name: mypod
...
```

To complete a manifest, most objects will have a spec and, once created, will also return a status:

```
apiVersion: v1
kind: Pod
metadata:
  name: mypod
spec:
  ...
status:
  ...
```

See Also

- Understanding Kubernetes Objects (*https://kubernetes.io/docs/concepts/overview/working-with-objects/kubernetes-objects/*)

6.3 Creating Namespaces to Avoid Name Collisions

Problem

You want to create two objects with the same name but want to avoid naming collisions.

Solution

Create namespaces and place your objects in different ones.

If you don't specify anything, objects will get created in the default namespace. Try creating a second namespace called my-app, as shown here, and list the existing namespaces. You will see the default namespace, two other namespaces that were created on startup (kube-system and kube-public), and the *my-app* namespace you just created:

```
$ kubectl create namespace my-app
namespace "my-app" created

$ kubectl get ns
NAME          STATUS   AGE
default       Active   30s
my-app        Active   1s
kube-public   Active   29s
kube-system   Active   30s
```

Alternatively, you can write a manifest to create your namespace. If you save the following manifest as *app.yaml*, you can then create the namespace with the `kubectl create -f app.yaml` command:

```
apiVersion: v1
kind: Namespace
metadata:
  name: my-app
```

Discussion

Attempting to start two objects with the same name in the same namespace (e.g., `default`) leads to a collision, and an error is returned by the Kubernetes API server. However, if you start the second object in a different namespace, the API server will create it:

```
$ kubectl run foobar --image=ghost:0.9
deployment "foobar" created

$ kubectl run foobar --image=nginx:1.13
Error from server (AlreadyExists): deployments.extensions "foobar" already exists

$ kubectl run foobar --image=nginx:1.13 --namespace foobar
deployment "foobar" created
```

This is because many API objects in Kubernetes are namespaced. The namespace they belong to is defined as part of the object's metadata.

The `kube-system` namespace is reserved for administrators, whereas the `kube-public` namespace (*http://bit.ly/kube-public*) is meant to store public objects available to any users of the cluster.

6.4 Setting Quotas Within a Namespace

Problem

You want to limit the resources available in a namespace—for example, the overall number of pods that can run in the namespace.

Solution

Use a `ResourceQuota` object to specify the limitations on a namespace basis:

```
$ cat resource-quota-pods.yaml
apiVersion: v1
kind: ResourceQuota
metadata:
```

```
  name: podquota
spec:
  hard:
    pods: "10"


$ kubectl create namespace my-app

$ kubectl create -f resource-quota-pods.yaml --namespace=my-app

$ kubectl describe resourcequota podquota --namespace=my-app
Name:            podquota
Namespace:       my-app
Resource         Used    Hard
--------         ----    ----
pods             0       10
```

Discussion

You can set a number of quotas on a per-namespace basis, including but not limited to pods, secrets, and config maps.

See Also

- Configure Quotas for API Objects (*https://kubernetes.io/docs/tasks/administer-cluster/quota-api-object/*)

6.5 Labeling an Object

Problem

You want to label an object in order to find it later on. The label can be used for further end-user queries (see Recipe 6.6) or in the context of system automation.

Solution

Use the `kubectl label` command. For example, to label a pod named `foobar` with the key/value pair `tier=frontend`, do this:

```
$ kubectl label pods foobar tier=frontend
```

 Check the complete help for the command (`kubectl label --help`). You can use it to find out how to remove labels, overwrite existing ones, and even label all resources in a namespace.

Discussion

In Kubernetes, you use labels to organize objects in a flexible, nonhierarchical manner. A label is a key/value pair without any predefined meaning for Kubernetes. In other words, the content of the key/value pair is not interpreted by the system. You can use labels to express membership (e.g., object X belongs to department ABC), environments (e.g., this service runs in production), or really anything you need to organize your objects. Note that labels do have restrictions concerning their length and allowed values.[2]

6.6 Using Labels for Queries

Problem

You want to query objects efficiently.

Solution

Use the `kubectl get --selector` command. For example, given the following pods:

```
$ kubectl get pods --show-labels
NAME                        READY   ...   LABELS
cockroachdb-0               1/1     ...   app=cockroachdb,
cockroachdb-1               1/1     ...   app=cockroachdb,
cockroachdb-2               1/1     ...   app=cockroachdb,
jump-1247516000-sz87w       1/1     ...   pod-template-hash=1247516000,run=jump
nginx-4217019353-462mb      1/1     ...   pod-template-hash=4217019353,run=nginx
nginx-4217019353-z3g8d      1/1     ...   pod-template-hash=4217019353,run=nginx
prom-2436944326-pr60g       1/1     ...   app=prom,pod-template-hash=2436944326
```

You can select the pods that belong to the CockroachDB app (`app=cockroachdb`):

```
$ kubectl get pods --selector app=cockroachdb
NAME            READY   STATUS    RESTARTS   AGE
cockroachdb-0   1/1     Running   0          17h
cockroachdb-1   1/1     Running   0          17h
cockroachdb-2   1/1     Running   0          17h
```

Discussion

Labels are part of an object's metadata. Any object in Kubernetes can be labeled. Labels are also used by Kubernetes itself for pod selection by deployments (see Recipe 4.1) and services (see Chapter 5).

---

2 Kubernetes, "Labels and Selectors: Syntax and character set" (*https://kubernetes.io/docs/concepts/overview/working-with-objects/labels/#syntax-and-character-set*).

Labels can be added manually with the kubectl label command (see Recipe 6.5), or you can define labels in an object manifest, like so:

```
apiVersion: v1
kind: Pod
metadata:
  name: foobar
  labels:
    tier: frontend
...
```

Once labels are present, you can list them with kubectl get, noting the following:

- -l is the short form of --selector and will query objects with a specified key=value pair.
- --show-labels will show all the labels of each object returned.
- -L will add a column to the results returned with the value of the specified label.
- Many object kinds support set-based querying, meaning you can state a query in a form like "must be labelled with X and/or Y." For example, kubectl get pods -l 'env in (production, development)' would give you pods that are in either the production or development environment.

With two pods running, one with label run=barfoo and the other with label run=foo bar, you would get outputs similar to the following:

```
$ kubectl get pods --show-labels
NAME                        READY   ...   LABELS
barfoo-76081199-h3gwx       1/1     ...   pod-template-hash=76081199,run=barfoo
foobar-1123019601-6x9w1     1/1     ...   pod-template-hash=1123019601,run=foobar

$ kubectl get pods -Lrun
NAME                        READY   ...   RUN
barfoo-76081199-h3gwx       1/1     ...   barfoo
foobar-1123019601-6x9w1     1/1     ...   foobar

$ kubectl get pods -l run=foobar
NAME                        READY   ...
foobar-1123019601-6x9w1     1/1     ...
```

See Also

- Kubernetes Labels documentation (*https://kubernetes.io/docs/concepts/overview/working-with-objects/labels/*)

6.7 Annotating a Resource with One Command

Problem

You want to annotate a resource with a generic, nonidentifying key/value pair, possibly using nonhuman readable data.

Solution

Use the kubectl annotate command:

```
$ kubectl annotate pods foobar \
description='something that you can use for automation'
```

Discussion

Annotations tend to be used for added automation of Kubernetes. For example, when you create a deployment with the kubectl run command and you forget to use the --record option, you will notice that the change-cause column in your rollout history (see Recipe 4.5) is empty. As of Kubernetes v1.6.0, to start recording the commands that cause changes to the deployment, you can annotate it with the kubernetes.io/change-cause key. Given a deployment foobar, you might annotate it with:

```
$ kubectl annotate deployment foobar \
kubernetes.io/change-cause="Reason for creating a new revision"
```

Subsequent changes to the deployment will be recorded.

## CHAPTER 7

Managing Specialized Workloads

In Chapter 4, we explored how to launch applications that are supposed to run forever, such as a web server or an app server. In this chapter, we will discuss workloads that are somewhat more specialized—for example, ones that launch terminating processes such as batch jobs, run pods on certain nodes, or manage stateful and noncloud native apps.

7.1 Running a Batch Job

Problem

You want to run a process that runs for a certain time to completion, such as a batch conversion, backup operation, or database schema upgrade.

Solution

Use a Kubernetes job resource to launch and supervise the pod(s) that will carry out the batch process.[1]

First, define the Kubernetes manifest for the job in a file called *counter-batch-job.yaml*:

```
apiVersion:        batch/v1
kind:              Job
metadata:
  name:            counter
spec:
```

---

[1] Kubernetes, "Jobs - Run to Completion" (*https://kubernetes.io/docs/concepts/workloads/controllers/jobs-run-to-completion/*).

```
    template:
      metadata:
        name:        counter
      spec:
        containers:
        - name:        counter
          image:       busybox
          command:
          - "sh"
          - "-c"
          - "for i in 1 2 3 ; do echo $i ; done"
        restartPolicy: Never
```

Then launch the job and have a look at its status:

```
$ kubectl create -f counter-batch-job.yaml
job "counter" created

$ kubectl get jobs
NAME      DESIRED   SUCCESSFUL   AGE
counter   1         1            22s

$ kubectl describe jobs/counter
Name:           counter
Namespace:      default
Selector:       controller-uid=634b9015-7f58-11e7-b58a-080027390640
Labels:         controller-uid=634b9015-7f58-11e7-b58a-080027390640
                job-name=counter
Annotations:    <none>
Parallelism:    1
Completions:    1
Start Time:     Sat, 12 Aug 2017 13:18:45 +0100
Pods Statuses:  0 Running / 1 Succeeded / 0 Failed
Pod Template:
  Labels:       controller-uid=634b9015-7f58-11e7-b58a-080027390640
                job-name=counter
  Containers:
   counter:
    Image:      busybox
    Port:       <none>
    Command:
      sh
      -c
      for i in 1 2 3 ; do echo $i ; done
    Environment:        <none>
    Mounts:             <none>
  Volumes:              <none>
Events:
  FirstSeen  ...  ...  ...  Type    Reason           Message
  ---------  ...  ...  ...  ------  ------           -------
  31s        ...  ...  ...  Normal  SuccessfulCreate  Created pod: counter-0pt20
```

Finally, you want to verify that it actually carried out the task (counting from 1 to 3):

```
$ kubectl logs jobs/counter
1
2
3
```

Indeed, as you can see, the `counter` job counted as expected.

If you don't need the job anymore, use `kubectl delete jobs/counter` to remove it.

7.2 Running a Task on a Schedule Within a Pod

Problem

You want to run a task on a specific schedule within a pod managed by Kubernetes.

Solution

Use Kubernetes `CronJob` objects. The `CronJob` object is a derivative of the more generic `Job` object (see Recipe 7.1).

You can periodically schedule a job by writing a manifest similar to the one shown here. In the `spec`, you see a `schedule` section that follows the crontab format. The `template` section describes the pod that will run and the command that will get executed (it prints the current date and time every hour to `stdout`):

```
apiVersion:           batch/v2alpha1
kind:                 CronJob
metadata:
  name:               hourly-date
spec:
  schedule:           "0 * * * *"
  jobTemplate:
    spec:
      template:
        spec:
          containers:
          - name:       date
            image:      busybox
            command:
              - "sh"
              - "-c"
              - "date"
          restartPolicy: OnFailure
```

See Also

- CronJob documentation (*https://kubernetes.io/docs/concepts/workloads/control lers/cron-jobs/*)

7.3 Running Infrastructure Daemons per Node

Problem

You want to launch an infrastructure daemon—for example, a log collector or monitoring agent—making sure that exactly one pod runs per node.

Solution

Use a DaemonSet to launch and supervise the daemon process. For example, to launch a Fluentd agent on each node in your cluster, create a file named *fluentd-daemonset.yaml* with the following content:

```
kind:              DaemonSet
apiVersion:        extensions/v1beta1
metadata:
  name:            fluentd
spec:
  template:
    metadata:
      labels:
        app:       fluentd
      name:        fluentd
    spec:
      containers:
      - name:      fluentd
        image:     gcr.io/google_containers/fluentd-elasticsearch:1.3
        env:
         - name:   FLUENTD_ARGS
           value:  -qq
        volumeMounts:
         - name:   varlog
           mountPath: /varlog
         - name:   containers
           mountPath: /var/lib/docker/containers
      volumes:
       - hostPath:
           path:   /var/log
         name:     varlog
       - hostPath:
           path:   /var/lib/docker/containers
         name:     containers
```

Now launch the `DaemonSet`, like so:

```
$ kubectl create -f fluentd-daemonset.yaml
daemonset "fluentd" created

$ kubectl get ds
NAME     DESIRED  CURRENT  READY  UP-TO-DATE  AVAILABLE  NODE-SELECTOR  AGE
fluentd  1        1        1      1           1          <none>         17s

$ kubectl describe ds/fluentd
Name:           fluentd
Selector:       app=fluentd
Node-Selector:  <none>
Labels:         app=fluentd
Annotations:    <none>
Desired Number of Nodes Scheduled: 1
Current Number of Nodes Scheduled: 1
Number of Nodes Scheduled with Up-to-date Pods: 1
Number of Nodes Scheduled with Available Pods: 1
Number of Nodes Misscheduled: 0
Pods Status:    1 Running / 0 Waiting / 0 Succeeded / 0 Failed
...
```

Discussion

Note that in the preceding output, because the command is executed on Minikube, you only see one pod running as there's only one node in this setup. If you had 15 nodes in your cluster, you'd have 15 pods overall with 1 pod per node running. You can also restrict the daemon to certain nodes using the `nodeSelector` section in the spec of the `DaemonSet` manifest.

7.4 Managing Stateful and Leader/Follower Apps

Problem

You want to run an app that requires that its pods have distinct, potentially different characteristics, such as a database where you have a leader handling reads and writes and several followers that only serve reads. You can't use deployments because they only supervise identical pods, and you need a supervisor that can deal with pods that are more like pets than cattle.

Solution

Use a `StatefulSet`, which enables workloads with unique network names, graceful deployment/scaling/termination, or persistent storage. For example, to run the popu-

---

lar scalable datastore CockroachDB, you can use the provided example,[2] which contains at its core the following `StatefulSet`:

```
apiVersion: apps/v1beta1
kind:                    StatefulSet
metadata:
  name:                  cockroachdb
spec:
  serviceName:           "cockroachdb"
  replicas:              3
  template:
    metadata:
      labels:
        app:             cockroachdb
    spec:
      initContainers:
      - name:            bootstrap
        image:           cockroachdb/cockroach-k8s-init:0.2
        imagePullPolicy: IfNotPresent
        args:
        - "-on-start=/on-start.sh"
        - "-service=cockroachdb"
        env:
        - name:          POD_NAMESPACE
          valueFrom:
            fieldRef:
              fieldPath: metadata.namespace
        volumeMounts:
        - name: datadir
          mountPath:     "/cockroach/cockroach-data"
      affinity:
        podAntiAffinity:
          preferredDuringSchedulingIgnoredDuringExecution:
          - weight: 100
            podAffinityTerm:
              labelSelector:
                matchExpressions:
                - key: app
                  operator:  In
                  values:
                  - cockroachdb
              topologyKey: kubernetes.io/hostname
      containers:
      - name:            cockroachdb
        image:           cockroachdb/cockroach:v1.0.3
        imagePullPolicy: IfNotPresent
        ports:
        - containerPort: 26257
```

---

2 Kubernetes cockroachdb example on GitHub, *cockroachdb-statefulset.yaml* (*https://github.com/kubernetes/ kubernetes/blob/master/examples/cockroachdb/cockroachdb-statefulset.yaml*).

```
            name: grpc
        - containerPort:      8080
          name: http
      volumeMounts:
      - name: datadir
        mountPath:            /cockroach/cockroach-data
      command:
        - "/bin/bash"
        - "-ecx"
        - |
          if [ ! "$(hostname)" == "cockroachdb-0" ] || \
             [ -e "/cockroach/cockroach-data/cluster_exists_marker" ]
          then
            CRARGS+=("--join" "cockroachdb-public")
          fi
          exec /cockroach/cockroach ${CRARGS[*]}
    terminationGracePeriodSeconds: 60
    volumes:
    - name:                   datadir
      persistentVolumeClaim:
        claimName:            datadir
  volumeClaimTemplates:
  - metadata:
      name:                   datadir
      annotations:
        volume.alpha.kubernetes.io/storage-class: anything
    spec:
      accessModes:
        - "ReadWriteOnce"
      resources:
        requests:
          storage:            1Gi
```

To launch it, do this:

```
$ curl -s -o cockroachdb-statefulset.yaml \
        https://raw.githubusercontent.com/kubernetes/kubernetes/master/ \
        examples/cockroachdb/cockroachdb-statefulset.yaml

$ curl -s -o crex.sh \
        https://raw.githubusercontent.com/kubernetes/kubernetes/master/ \
        examples/cockroachdb/minikube.sh

$ ./crex.sh
+ kubectl delete statefulsets,persistentvolumes,persistentvolumeclaims,services...
...
+ kubectl create -f -
persistentvolumeclaim "datadir-cockroachdb-3" created
+ kubectl create -f cockroachdb-statefulset.yaml
service "cockroachdb-public" created
service "cockroachdb" created
poddisruptionbudget "cockroachdb-budget" created
statefulset "cockroachdb" created
```

Now you can see the `StatefulSet` object created along with the pods in the Kubernetes dashboard (Figure 7-1).

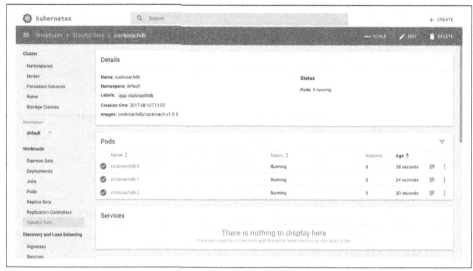

Figure 7-1. Screenshot of a StatefulSet

Discussion

Originally, what is now known in Kubernetes as a `StatefulSet` was called a `PetSet`. This should give you an idea of what the motivation was. In Kubernetes 1.7, the `StatefulSet` became a beta feature, which means that the API is not going to change anymore; only UX fixes are to be expected. A `StatefulSet` is a controller that provides unique identities to the pods it is supervising. Note that, as a safety measure, deleting a `StatefulSet` will not delete the volumes associated with it.

Another use case for a `StatefulSet`, found quite often in the wild, is to run an app that was not written with Kubernetes in mind. Such apps are sometimes called *legacy apps*, from a Kubernetes perspective. We will refer to these apps as non-cloud-native apps going forward. Using `StatefulSet` is a good way to supervise such an app.

See Also

- StatefulSet Basics (*https://kubernetes.io/docs/tutorials/stateful-application/basic-stateful-set/*)
- Run a Replicated Stateful Application (*https://kubernetes.io/docs/tasks/run-application/run-replicated-stateful-application/*)
- Example: Deploying Cassandra with Stateful Sets (*https://kubernetes.io/docs/tutorials/stateful-application/cassandra/*)

- Kubernetes Redis as Stateful Set with Sentinel (*https://github.com/corybuecker/redis-stateful-set*)

- Oleg Chunikhin's article "How to Run a MongoDb Replica Set on Kubernetes PetSet or StatefulSet" (*https://www.linkedin.com/pulse/how-run-mongodb-replica-set-kubernetes-petset-oleg-chunikhin*)

- The Hacker News discussion on StatefulSets (*https://news.ycombinator.com/item?id=13225183*)

7.5 Influencing Pods' Startup Behavior

Problem

Your pod depends on some other service being available in order to function properly.

Solution

Use init containers (*https://kubernetes.io/docs/concepts/workloads/pods/init-containers/*) to influence the startup behavior of a pod.

Imagine you want to launch an nginx web server that depends on a backend service to serve content. You therefore want to make sure that the nginx pod only starts up once the backend service is up and running.

First, create the backend service the web server depends on:

```
$ kubectl run backend --image=mhausenblas/simpleservice:0.5.0
deployment "backend" created

$ kubectl expose deployment backend --port=80 --target-port=9876
```

Then you can use the following manifest, *nginx-init-container.yaml*, to launch the nginx instance and make sure it starts up only when the backend deployment serves data:

```
kind:                Deployment
apiVersion:          apps/v1beta1
metadata:
  name:              nginx
spec:
  replicas:          1
  template:
    metadata:
      labels:
        app:         nginx
    spec:
      containers:
```

```
  - name:           webserver
    image:          nginx
    ports:
    - containerPort: 80
  initContainers:
  - name:           checkbackend
    image:          busybox
    command:        ['sh', '-c', 'until nslookup backend.default.svc; do echo
                      "Waiting for backend to come up"; sleep 3; done; echo
                      "Backend is up, ready to launch web server"']
```

Now you can launch the `nginx` deployment and verify whether the init container has done its job by looking at the logs of the pod it is supervising:

```
$ kubectl create -f nginx-init-container.yaml
deployment "nginx" created

$ kubectl get po
NAME                       READY   STATUS    RESTARTS   AGE
backend-853383893-2g0gs    1/1     Running   0          43m
nginx-2101406530-jwghn     1/1     Running   0          10m

$ kubectl logs nginx-2101406530-jwghn -c checkbackend
Server:     10.0.0.10
Address 1:  10.0.0.10 kube-dns.kube-system.svc.cluster.local

Name:       backend.default.svc
Address 1:  10.0.0.46 backend.default.svc.cluster.local
Backend is up, ready to launch web server
```

As you can see, the command in the init container indeed worked as planned.

## CHAPTER 8

Volumes and Configuration Data

A *volume* in Kubernetes is a directory accessible to all containers running in a pod, with the additional guarantee that the data is preserved across restarts of individual containers.

Depending on what is backing the volume and potentially additional semantics present, we differentiate the types of volumes:

- *Node-local* volumes, such as `emptyDir` or `hostPath`
- Generic *networked* volumes, such as `nfs`, `glusterfs`, or `cephfs`
- *Cloud provider–specific* volumes, such as `awsElasticBlockStore`, `azureDisk`, or `gcePersistentDisk`
- *Special-purpose* volumes, such as `secret` or `gitRepo`

Which volume type you choose depends entirely on your use case. For example, for a temporary scratch space, an `emptyDir` would be fine, but when you need to make sure your data survives node failures you'll want to look into networked volumes, or cloud-provider–specific ones if you run Kubernetes in a public cloud setting.

8.1 Exchanging Data Between Containers via a Local Volume

Problem

You have two or more containers running in a pod and want to be able to exchange data via filesystem operations.

Solution

Use a local volume of type `emptyDir`.

The starting point is the following pod manifest, *exchangedata.yaml*, which has two containers (`c1` and `c2`) that each mount the local volume `xchange` into their filesystem, using different mount points:

```
apiVersion:        v1
kind:              Pod
metadata:
  name:            sharevol
spec:
  containers:
  - name:          c1
    image:         centos:7
    command:
      - "bin/bash"
      - "-c"
      - "sleep 10000"
    volumeMounts:
      - name:        xchange
        mountPath:   "/tmp/xchange"
  - name:          c2
    image:         centos:7
    command:
      - "bin/bash"
      - "-c"
      - "sleep 10000"
    volumeMounts:
      - name:        xchange
        mountPath:   "/tmp/data"
  volumes:
  - name:          xchange
    emptyDir:      {}
```

Now you can launch the pod, exec into it, create data from one container, and read it out from the other one:

```
$ kubectl create -f exchangedata.yaml
pod "sharevol" created

$ kubectl exec sharevol -c c1 -i -t -- bash
[root@sharevol /]# mount | grep xchange
/dev/vda1 on /tmp/xchange type ext4 (rw,relatime,data=ordered)
[root@sharevol /]# echo 'some data' > /tmp/xchange/data
[root@sharevol /]# exit

$ kubectl exec sharevol -c c2 -i -t -- bash
[root@sharevol /]# mount | grep /tmp/data
/dev/vda1 on /tmp/data type ext4 (rw,relatime,data=ordered)
```

```
[root@sharevol /]# cat /tmp/data/data
some data
```

Discussion

A local volume is backed by the node the pod and its containers are running on. If the node goes down or you have to carry out maintenance on the node (see Recipe 12.8), then the local volume is gone and all the data is lost.

There are some use cases where local volumes are fine—for example, for some scratch space or when the canonical state is obtained from somewhere else, such as an S3 bucket—but in general you'll want to use a volume backed by networked storage (see Recipe 8.6).

See Also

- Kubernetes Volumes documentation (*https://kubernetes.io/docs/concepts/storage/volumes/*)

8.2 Passing an API Access Key to a Pod Using a Secret

Problem

As an admin, you want to provide your developers with an API access key in a secure way; that is, without sharing it in clear text in your Kubernetes manifests.

Solution

Use a local volume of type `secret` (*https://kubernetes.io/docs/concepts/storage/volumes/#secret*).

Let's say you want to give your developers access to an external service that is accessible via the passphrase open sesame.

First, create a text file called *passphrase* that holds the passphrase:

```
$ echo -n "open sesame" > ./passphrase
```

Next, create the secret (*https://kubernetes.io/docs/concepts/configuration/secret/*), using the *passphrase* file:

```
$ kubectl create secret generic pp --from-file=./passphrase
secret "pp" created

$ kubectl describe secrets/pp
Name:        pp
Namespace:   default
```

```
Labels:          <none>
Annotations:     <none>

Type:    Opaque

Data
====
passphrase:      11 bytes
```

From an admin point of view, you're all set now and it's time for your developers to consume the secret. So let's switch hats and assume you're a developer and want to use the passphrase from within a pod.

You would consume the secret, for example, by mounting it as a volume into your pod and then reading it out as a normal file. Create the pod and mount the volume now:

```
apiVersion:      v1
kind:            Pod
metadata:
  name:          ppconsumer
spec:
  containers:
  - name:        shell
    image:       busybox
    command:
      - "sh"
      - "-c"
      - "mount | grep access  && sleep 3600"
    volumeMounts:
      - name:      passphrase
        mountPath: "/tmp/access"
        readOnly:  true
  volumes:
  - name:        passphrase
    secret:
      secretName:  pp
```

Now launch the pod and have a look at its logs, where you would expect to see the pp secret file mounted as */tmp/access/passphrase*:

```
$ kubectl create -f ppconsumer.yaml
pod "ppconsumer" created

$ kubectl logs ppconsumer
tmpfs on /tmp/access type tmpfs (ro,relatime)
```

To access the passphrase from within the running container, simply read out the *passphrase* file in */tmp/access*, like so:

```
$ kubectl exec ppconsumer -i -t -- sh

/ # cat /tmp/access/passphrase
open sesame
```

Discussion

Secrets exist in the context of a namespace, so you need to take that into account when setting them up and/or consuming them.

You can access a secret from a container running in a pod via one of the following:

- A volume (as shown in the Solution, where the content is stored in a `tmpfs` volume)
- An environment variable (*https://kubernetes.io/docs/concepts/configuration/secret/#using-secrets-as-environment-variables*)

Also, note that the size of a secret is limited to 1 MB.

In addition to user-defined secrets, Kubernetes automatically creates secrets for service accounts to access the API. For example, with Prometheus installed (see Recipe 11.6), you'd see something like Figure 8-1 in the Kubernetes dashboard.

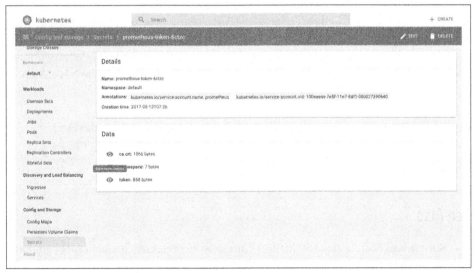

Figure 8-1. Screenshot of the Prometheus service account secret

kubectl create secret deals with three types of secrets and, depending on your use case, you might want to choose different ones:

- The docker-registry type is for use with a Docker registry.

- The generic type is what we used in the Solution; it creates a secret from a local file, directory, or literal value (you need to base64-encode it yourself).

- With tls you can create, for example, a secure SSL certificate for ingress.

kubectl describe doesn't show the content of the secret in the plain text. This avoids "over-the-shoulder" password grabs. You can, however, easily decode it manually since it's not encrypted—only base64-encoded:

```
$ kubectl get secret pp -o yaml | \
  grep passphrase | \
  cut -d":" -f 2 | \
  awk '{$1=$1};1' | \
  base64 --decode
open sesame
```

In this command, the first line retrieves a YAML representation of the secret, and the second line with the grep pulls out the line passphrase: b3BlbiBzZXNhbWU= (note the leading whitespace here). Then, the cut extracts the content of the passphrase, and the awk command gets rid of the leading whitespace. Finally, the base64 command turns it into the original data again.

Prior to Kubernetes 1.7, the API server stored secrets as plain text in etcd. Now you have the option to encrypt them using the --experimental-encryption-provider-config option when launching the kube-apiserver.

See Also

- Kubernetes Secrets documentation (*https://kubernetes.io/docs/concepts/configuration/secret/*)

- Encrypting Secret Data at Rest (*https://kubernetes.io/docs/tasks/administer-cluster/encrypt-data/*)

8.3 Providing Configuration Data to an Application

Problem

You want to provide configuration data to an application without storing it in the container image or hardcoding it into the pod specification.

Solution

Use a config map. These are first-class Kubernetes resources with which you can provide configuration data to a pod via environment variables or a file.

Let's say you want to create a configuration with the key `siseversion` and the value `0.9`. It's as simple as this:

```
$ kubectl create configmap siseconfig --from-literal=siseversion=0.9
configmap "siseconfig" created
```

Now you can use the config map in a deployment—say, in a manifest file called *cmapp.yaml* with the following content:

```
apiVersion:              extensions/v1beta1
kind:                    Deployment
metadata:
  name:                  cmapp
spec:
  replicas:              1
  template:
    metadata:
      labels:
        app:             cmapp
    spec:
      containers:
      - name:            sise
        image:           mhausenblas/simpleservice:0.5.0
        ports:
        - containerPort: 9876
        env:
        - name:          SIMPLE_SERVICE_VERSION
          valueFrom:
            configMapKeyRef:
              name:      siseconfig
              key:       siseversion
```

We've just shown how to pass in the configuration as an environment variable. However, you can also mount it into the pod as a file, using a volume.

Suppose you have the following config file, *example.cfg*:

```
debug: true
home: ~/abc
```

You can create a config map that holds the config file, as follows:

```
$ kubectl create configmap configfile --from-file=example.cfg
```

Now you can use the config map just as you would any other volume. The following is the manifest file for a pod named oreilly; it uses the busybox image and just sleeps for 3,600 seconds. In the volumes section, there is a volume named oreilly which uses the config map configfile that we just created. This volume is then mounted at the path /oreilly inside the container. Hence, the file will be accessible within the pod:

```
apiVersion:         v1
kind:               Pod
metadata:
  name:             oreilly
spec:
  containers:
  - image:          busybox
    command:
      - sleep
      - "3600"
    volumeMounts:
    - mountPath:    /oreilly
      name:         oreilly
    name:           busybox
  volumes:
  - name:           oreilly
    configMap:
      name:         configfile
```

After creating the pod, you can verify that the *example.cfg* file is indeed inside it:

```
$ kubectl exec -ti oreilly -- ls -l /oreilly
total 0
lrwxrwxrwx   1 root   root   18 Dec 16 19:36 example.cfg -> ..data/example.cfg

$ kubectl exec -ti oreilly -- cat /oreilly/example.cfg
debug: true
home: ~/abc
```

For a complete example of how to create a config map from a file, see Recipe 11.6.

See Also

- Configure a Pod to Use a ConfigMap (*https://kubernetes.io/docs/tasks/configure-pod-container/configure-pod-configmap/*)

8.4 Using a Persistent Volume with Minikube

Problem

You don't want to lose data on a disk your container uses—that is, you want to make sure it survives a restart of the hosting pod.

Solution

Use a persistent volume (PV). In the case of Minikube, you can create a PV of type hostPath and mount it just like a normal volume into the container's filesystem.

First, define the PV hostpathpv in a manifest called *hostpath-pv.yaml*:

```
kind:               PersistentVolume
apiVersion:         v1
metadata:
  name:             hostpathpv
  labels:
    type:           local
spec:
  storageClassName: manual
  capacity:
    storage:        1Gi
  accessModes:
  - ReadWriteOnce
  hostPath:
    path:           "/tmp/pvdata"
```

Before you can create the PV, however, you need to prepare the directory */tmp/pvdata* on the node—that is, the Minikube instance itself. You can get into the node where the Kubernetes cluster is running using minikube ssh:

```
$ minikube ssh

$ mkdir /tmp/pvdata && \
  echo 'I am content served from a delicious persistent volume' > / \
  tmp/pvdata/index.html

$ cat /tmp/pvdata/index.html
I am content served from a delicious persistent volume

$ exit
```

Now that you've prepared the directory on the node, you can create the PV from the manifest file *hostpath-pv.yaml*:

```
$ kubectl create -f hostpath-pv.yaml
persistentvolume "hostpathpv" created

$ kubectl get pv
```

```
NAME          CAPACITY   ACCESSMODES   RECLAIMPOLICY   STATUS       ...   ...   ...
hostpathpv    1Gi        RWO           Retain          Available    ...   ...   ...

$ kubectl describe pv/hostpathpv
Name:          hostpathpv
Labels:        type=local
Annotations:   <none>
StorageClass:  manual
Status:        Available
Claim:
Reclaim Policy: Retain
Access Modes:  RWO
Capacity:      1Gi
Message:
Source:
    Type:      HostPath (bare host directory volume)
    Path:      /tmp/pvdata
Events:        <none>
```

Up to this point, you would carry out these steps in an admin role. You would define PVs and make them available to developers on the Kubernetes cluster.

Now you're in a position to use the PV in a pod, from a developer's perspective. This is done via a *persistent volume claim* (PVC), so called because, well, you literally claim a PV that fulfills certain characteristics, such as size or storage class.

Create a manifest file called *pvc.yaml* that defines a PVC, asking for 200 MB of space:

```
kind:                PersistentVolumeClaim
apiVersion:          v1
metadata:
  name:              mypvc
spec:
  storageClassName: manual
  accessModes:
  - ReadWriteOnce
  resources:
    requests:
      storage:       200Mi
```

Next, launch the PVC and verify its state:

```
$ kubectl create -f pvc.yaml
persistentvolumeclaim "mypvc" created

$ kubectl get pv
NAME          CAPACITY   ACCESSMODES   ...   STATUS   CLAIM           STORAGECLASS
hostpathpv    1Gi        RWO           ...   Bound    default/mypvc   manual
```

Note that the status of the PV hostpathpv has changed from Available to Bound.

Finally, it's time to consume the data from the PV in a container, this time via a deployment that mounts it in the filesystem. So, create a file called *nginx-using-pv.yaml* with the following content:

```
kind:                        Deployment
apiVersion:                  extensions/v1beta1
metadata:
  name:                      nginx-with-pv
spec:
  replicas:                  1
  template:
    metadata:
      labels:
        app:                 nginx
    spec:
      containers:
      - name:                webserver
        image:               nginx
        ports:
        - containerPort:     80
        volumeMounts:
        - mountPath:         "/usr/share/nginx/html"
          name:              webservercontent
      volumes:
      - name:                webservercontent
        persistentVolumeClaim:
          claimName:         mypvc
```

And launch the deployment, like so:

```
$ kubectl create -f nginx-using-pv.yaml
deployment "nginx-with-pv" created

$ kubectl get pvc
NAME    STATUS  VOLUME      CAPACITY  ACCESSMODES  STORAGECLASS  AGE
mypvc   Bound   hostpathpv  1Gi       RWO          manual        12m
```

As you can see, the PV is in use via the PVC you created earlier.

To verify that the data actually has arrived, you could now create a service (see Recipe 5.1) along with an `ingress` object (see Recipe 5.5) and then access it like so:

```
$ curl -k -s https://192.168.99.100/web
I am content served from a delicious persistent volume
```

Well done! You've (as an admin) provisioned a persistent volume and (as a developer) claimed it via a persistent volume claim, and used it from a deployment in a pod by mounting it into the container filesystem.

Discussion

In the Solution, we used a persistent volume of type `hostPath`. In a production setting, you would not want to use this but rather ask your cluster administrator nicely to provision a networked volume backed by NFS or an Amazon Elastic Block Store (EBS) volume to make sure your data sticks around and survives single-node failures.

 Remember that PVs are cluster-wide resources; that is, they are not namespaced. However, PVCs are namespaced. You can claim PVs from specific namespaces using namespaced PVCs.

See Also

- Kubernetes Persistent Volumes documentation (*https://kubernetes.io/docs/concepts/storage/persistent-volumes/*)
- Configure a Pod to Use a PersistentVolume for Storage (*https://kubernetes.io/docs/tasks/configure-pod-container/configure-persistent-volume-storage/*)

8.5 Understanding Data Persistency on Minikube

Problem

You want to use Minikube to understand how you could deploy a stateful application in Kubernetes. Specifically, you would like to deploy a MySQL database.

Solution

Use a `PersistentVolumeClaim` object (see Recipe 8.4) in your pod definition and/or the template for your database.

First you need to make a request for a specific amount of storage. The following *data.yaml* manifest makes a request for 1 GB of storage.

```
kind:            PersistentVolumeClaim
apiVersion:      v1
metadata:
  name:          data
spec:
  accessModes:
    - ReadWriteOnce
  resources:
    requests:
      storage: 1Gi
```

On Minikube, create this PVC and immediately see how a persistent volume is created to match this claim:

```
$ kubectl create -f data.yaml

$ kubectl get pvc
NAME   STATUS   VOLUME                                    CAPACITY ...  ...  ...
data   Bound    pvc-da58c85c-e29a-11e7-ac0b-080027fcc0e7  1Gi        ...  ...  ...

$ kubectl get pv
NAME                                      CAPACITY ...  ...  ...  ...  ...
pvc-da58c85c-e29a-11e7-ac0b-080027fcc0e7  1Gi        ...  ...  ...  ...  ...
```

You are now ready to use this claim in your pod. In the volumes section, define a volume by name with a PVC type and a reference to the PVC you just created. In the volumeMounts field, you'll mount this volume at a specific path inside your container. For MySQL, you mount it at /var/lib/mysql:

```
apiVersion:      v1
kind:            Pod
metadata:
  name:          db
spec:
  containers:
  - image:       mysql:5.5
    name:        db
    volumeMounts:
    - mountPath: /var/lib/mysql
      name:      data
    env:
      - name:    MYSQL_ROOT_PASSWORD
        value:   root
  volumes:
  - name:        data
    persistentVolumeClaim:
      claimName: data
```

Discussion

Minkube is configured out of the box with a default storage class that defines a default persistent volume provisioner. This means that when a persistent volume claim is created, Kubernetes will dynamically create a matching persistent volume to fill that claim.

This is what happened in the Solution. Once you created the data PVC, Kubernetes automatically created a PV to match that claim. If you look a bit deeper at the default storage class on Minikube, you will see the provisioner type:

```
$ kubectl get storageclass
NAME                PROVISIONER
standard (default)  k8s.io/minikube-hostpath

$ kubectl get storageclass standard -o yaml
apiVersion: storage.k8s.io/v1
kind: StorageClass
...
provisioner: k8s.io/minikube-hostpath
reclaimPolicy: Delete
```

This specific storage class is using a storage provisioner that creates persistent volumes of type hostPath. You can see this by looking at the manifest of the PV that got created to match the claim you created previously:

```
$ kubectl get pv
NAME                                             CAPACITY  ... CLAIM          ...
pvc-da58c85c-e29a-11e7-ac0b-080027fcc0e7  1Gi       ... default/foobar ...

$ kubectl get pv pvc-da58c85c-e29a-11e7-ac0b-080027fcc0e7 -o yaml
apiVersion: v1
kind: PersistentVolume
...
  hostPath:
    path: /tmp/hostpath-provisioner/pvc-da58c85c-e29a-11e7-ac0b-080027fcc0e7
    type: ""
...
```

To verify that the host volume created holds the database data, you can connect to Minikube and list the files in the directory:

```
$ minikube ssh
```

```
$ ls -l /tmp/hostpath-provisioner/pvc-da58c85c-e29a-11e7-ac0b-080027fcc0e7
total 28688
-rw-rw---- 1 999 999        2 Dec 16 20:02 data.pid
-rw-rw---- 1 999 999  5242880 Dec 16 20:02 ib_logfile0
-rw-rw---- 1 999 999  5242880 Dec 16 20:02 ib_logfile1
-rw-rw---- 1 999 999 18874368 Dec 16 20:02 ibdata1
drwx------ 2 999 999     4096 Dec 16 20:02 mysql
drwx------ 2 999 999     4096 Dec 16 20:03 oreilly
drwx------ 2 999 999     4096 Dec 16 20:02 performance_schema
```

Indeed, you now have data persistence. If the pod dies (or you delete it), your data will still be available.

In general, `storage classes` allow the cluster administrator to define the various types of storage they might provide. For the developers, it abstracts the type of storage and lets them use PVC without having to worry about the storage provider itself.

See Also

- Persistent Volumes documentation (*https://kubernetes.io/docs/concepts/storage/persistent-volumes/#persistentvolumeclaims*)
- Storage Classes documentation (*https://kubernetes.io/docs/concepts/storage/storage-classes/*)

8.6 Dynamically Provisioning Persistent Storage on GKE

Problem

Rather than manually provisioning persistent volumes with persistent volume claims like in Recipe 8.4, you want to automate the process—that is, dynamically provision PVs based on storage or pricing requirements.

Solution

For GKE, follow the steps outlined in the blog post by Saad Ali "Dynamic Provisioning and Storage Classes in Kubernetes" (*http://blog.kubernetes.io/2016/10/dynamic-provisioning-and-storage-in-kubernetes.html*).

Discussion

In general, the workflow to provision and claim PVs is as shown in Figure 8-2.

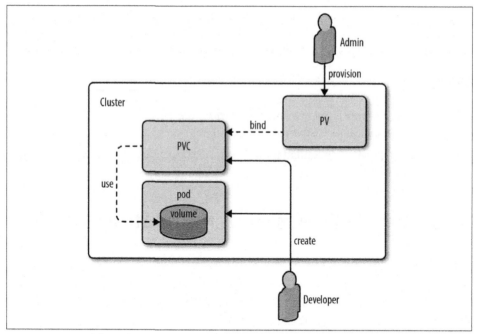

Figure 8-2. Workflow for provisioning and claiming persistent volumes

The workflow involves admins and developers coordinating available types and sizes of volumes. With dynamic provisioning, this workflow can be streamlined.

## CHAPTER 9

Scaling

In Kubernetes, scaling can mean different things to different users. We distinguish between two cases:

- *Cluster scaling*, sometimes called infrastructure-level scaling, refers to the (automated) process of adding or removing worker nodes based on cluster utilization.

- *Application-level scaling*, sometimes called pod scaling, refers to the (automated) process of manipulating pod characteristics based on a variety of metrics, from low-level signals such as CPU utilization to higher-level ones, such as HTTP requests served per second, for a given pod. Two kinds of pod-level scalers exist:

  — Horizontal Pod Autoscalers (HPAs), which increase or decrease the number of pod replicas depending on certain metrics.

  — Vertical Pod Autoscalers (VPAs), which increase or decrease the resource requirements of containers running in a pod. Since VPAs are still under development as of January 2018, we will not discuss them here. If you're interested in this topic, you can read about them in Michael's blog post "Container resource consumption—too important to ignore" (*https://hackernoon.com/container-resource-consumption-too-important-to-ignore-7484609a3bb7*).

In the chapter, we first examine cluster-level scaling for AWS and GKE, then discuss app-level scaling with HPAs.

9.1 Scaling a Deployment

Problem

You have a deployment and want to scale it horizontally.

Solution

Use the `kubectl scale` command to scale out a deployment.

Let's reuse the `fancyapp` deployment from Recipe 4.4, with five replicas. If it's not running yet, create it with `kubectl create -f fancyapp.yaml`.

Now suppose that the load has decreased and you don't need five replicas anymore; three is enough. To scale the deployment down to three replicas, do this:

```
$ kubectl get deploy fancyapp
NAME        DESIRED   CURRENT   UP-TO-DATE   AVAILABLE   AGE
fancyapp    5         5         5            5           9m

$ kubectl scale deployment fancyapp --replicas=3
deployment "fancyapp" scaled

$ kubectl get deploy fancyapp
NAME        DESIRED   CURRENT   UP-TO-DATE   AVAILABLE   AGE
fancyapp    3         3         3            3           10m
```

Rather than manually scaling a deployment, you can automate this process; see Recipe 9.4 for an example.

9.2 Automatically Resizing a Cluster in GKE

Problem

You want your GKE cluster to automatically grow or shrink in terms of the number of nodes, depending on the utilization.

Solution

Use the GKE Cluster Autoscaler. This recipe assumes you've got the `gcloud` command installed and the environment set up (i.e., you've created a project and enabled billing).

First, create a cluster with one worker node and make sure you can access it with `kubectl`:

```
$ gcloud container clusters create --num-nodes=1 supersizeme
Creating cluster supersizeme...done.
Created [https://container.googleapis.com/v1/projects/k8s-cookbook/zones/...].
kubeconfig entry generated for supersizeme.
NAME          ZONE            MASTER_VERSION   MASTER_IP        ...   STATUS
supersizeme   europe-west2-b  1.7.8-gke.0      35.189.116.207   ...   RUNNING

$ gcloud container clusters get-credentials supersizeme --zone europe-west2-b \
                                                        --project k8s-cookbook
```

Next, enable cluster autoscaling:

```
$ gcloud beta container clusters update supersizeme --enable-autoscaling \
                                          --min-nodes=1 --max-nodes=3 \
                                          --zone=europe-west2-b \
                                          --node-pool=default-pool
```

Note that if you haven't enabled the `beta` command group you will be prompted in this step for permission to install it.

At this point in time, when looking at the Google Cloud console you should see something like what is shown in Figure 9-1.

Figure 9-1. Screenshot of the Google Cloud console, showing the initial cluster size of one node

Now, launch 15 pods using a deployment. This will generate enough load to trigger the cluster autoscaling:

```
$ kubectl run ghost --image=ghost:0.9 --replicas=15
```

You should now have a cluster of three nodes, as depicted in Figure 9-2.

Figure 9-2. Screenshot of the Google Cloud console, showing the resulting cluster scaled to three nodes

Figure 9-3 shows you see the entire interaction:

- In the upper-left session you see the load (the 15 pods created, triggering the cluster scaling event).

- In the upper-right session you see the gcloud command, enabling the cluster autoscaling.

- In the bottom session you see the output of the kubectl get nodes --watch command, showing the current nodes available.

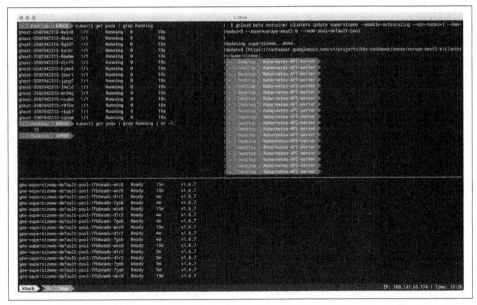

Figure 9-3. Screenshot of the terminal sessions, showing the cluster autoscaling in action

Note that all nodes in the node pool should have the same capacity, labels, and system pods running on them. Also, check that your quota is big enough when specifying the maximum settings for the node pool.

Don't forget to do `gcloud container clusters delete supersizeme` when you're done; otherwise, you'll keep paying for the cluster resources.

See Also

- Cluster Autoscaler (*https://github.com/kubernetes/autoscaler/tree/master/cluster-autoscaler*) in the *kubernetes/autoscaler* repo
- Cluster Autoscaler (*https://cloud.google.com/container-engine/docs/cluster-autoscaler*) in the GKE docs

9.3 Automatically Resizing a Cluster in AWS

Problem

You want your Kubernetes cluster running in AWS EC2 to automatically grow or shrink in terms of the number of nodes, depending on the utilization.

Solution

Use the AWS Cluster Autoscaler (*https://github.com/kubernetes/charts/tree/master/stable/cluster-autoscaler*), a Helm package leveraging AWS autoscaling groups. If you haven't installed Helm yet, then check out Recipe 14.1 first.

9.4 Using Horizontal Pod Autoscaling on GKE

Problem

You want to automatically increase or decrease the number of pods in a deployment, depending on the load present.

Solution

Use a Horizontal Pod Autoscaler, as described here.

First, create an app—a PHP environment and server—that you can use as the target of the HPA:

```
$ kubectl run appserver --image=gcr.io/google_containers/hpa-example \
                        --requests=cpu=200m --expose --port=80
service "appserver" created
  |NAME   ZONE          MASTER_VERSION
deployment "appserver" created
```

Next, create an HPA and define the trigger parameter --cpu-percent=40, which means that the CPU utilization should not go over 40%:

```
$ kubectl autoscale deployment appserver --cpu-percent=40 --min=1 --max=5
deployment "appserver" autoscaled

$ kubectl get hpa --watch
NAME        REFERENCE             TARGETS          MINPODS  MAXPODS  REPLICAS  AGE
appserver  Deployment/appserver  <unknown> / 40%  1        5        0         14s
```

In a second terminal session, keep an eye on the deployment:

```
$ kubectl get deploy appserver --watch
```

And finally, in a third terminal session, launch the load generator:

```
$ kubectl run -i -t loadgen --image=busybox /bin/sh
If you don't see a command prompt, try pressing enter.

/ # while true; do wget -q -O- http://appserver.default.svc.cluster.local; done
```

Since there are three terminal sessions involved in parallel, an overview of the whole situation is provided in Figure 9-4.

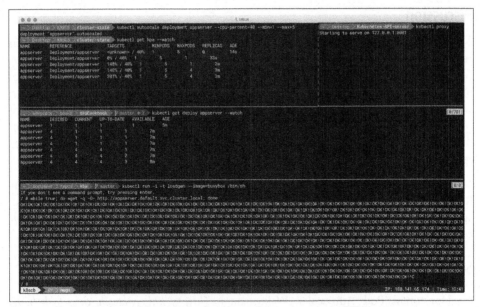

Figure 9-4. Screenshot of the terminal sessions for setting up an HPA

In Figure 9-5 you can see the effect of the HPA on the `appserver` deployment, this time showing the Kubernetes dashboard.

Figure 9-5. Screenshot of the Kubernetes dashboard, showing the effect of an HPA

Discussion

The autoscaling described here is the automatic increase or decrease of the number of replicas through the HPA controller, which can be influenced through an HPA resource. The controller, part of the Kubernetes controller manager in the control plane, checks pod metrics via cAdvisor instances running on each node in the cluster, which then get aggregated by Heapster. The HPA controller calculates the number of replicas required to meet the target metric defined in the HPA resource.[1] Based on this calculation, the HPA controller then adapts the replicas on the target resource (e.g., deployment).

Note that autoscaling can be tricky, and adjusting low-level metrics such as CPU or RAM utilization might not have the expected impact. If you can, try using application-level custom metrics (*https://blog.openshift.com/kubernetes-1-8-now-custom-metrics/*).

See Also

- Horizontal Pod Autoscaler Walkthrough (*https://kubernetes.io/docs/tasks/run-application/horizontal-pod-autoscale-walkthrough/*)

- Jerzy Szczepkowski and Marcin Wielgus's blog post "Autoscaling in Kubernetes" (*http://blog.kubernetes.io/2016/07/autoscaling-in-kubernetes.html*)

- Autoscaling demo in GKE (*https://github.com/mhausenblas/k8s-autoscale*)

---

[1] Kubernetes community on GitHub, "Autoscaling Algorithm" (*https://github.com/kubernetes/community/blob/master/contributors/design-proposals/autoscaling/horizontal-pod-autoscaler.md#autoscaling-algorithm*).

## CHAPTER 10

Security

Running applications in Kubernetes comes with a shared responsibility between developers and ops folks to ensure that attack vectors are minimized, least-privileges principles are followed, and access to resources is clearly defined. In this chapter, we will present recipes that you can, and should, use to make sure your cluster and apps run securely. The recipes in this chapter cover:

- The role and usage of service accounts
- Role-Based Access Control (RBAC)
- Defining a pod's security context

10.1 Providing a Unique Identity for an Application

Problem

You want to provide an application with a unique identity in order to control access to resources on a fine-grained level.

Solution

Create a service account and use it in a pod specification.

To begin, create a new service account called myappsa and have a closer look at it:

```
$ kubectl create serviceaccount myappsa
serviceaccount "myappsa" created

$ kubectl describe sa myappsa
Name:           myappsa
Namespace:      default
```

```
Labels:          <none>
Annotations:     <none>

Image pull secrets:    <none>

Mountable secrets:     myappsa-token-rr6jc

Tokens:                myappsa-token-rr6jc
$ kubectl describe secret myappsa-token-rr6jc
Name:          myappsa-token-rr6jc
Namespace:     default
Labels:        <none>
Annotations:   kubernetes.io/service-account.name=myappsa
               kubernetes.io/service-account.uid=0baa3df5-c474-11e7-8f08...

Type:    kubernetes.io/service-account-token

Data
====
ca.crt:       1066 bytes
namespace:    7 bytes
token:        eyJhbGciOiJSUzI1NiIsInR5cCI6IkpXVCJ9 ...
```

You can use this service account in a pod, like so:

```
kind:           Pod
apiVersion:     v1
metadata:
  name:         myapp
spec:
  serviceAccountName: myappsa
  containers:
  - name:       main
    image:      centos:7
    command:
      - "bin/bash"
      - "-c"
      - "sleep 10000"
```

You can then verify whether the service account myappsa has been properly used by
your pod by running:

```
$ kubectl exec myapp -c main \
      cat  /var/run/secrets/kubernetes.io/serviceaccount/token \
      eyJhbGciOiJSUzI1NiIsInR5cCI6IkpXVCJ9 ...
```

Indeed, the myappsa service account token has been mounted in the expected place in
the pod and can be used going forward.

While a service account on its own is not super useful, it forms the basis for fine-
grained access control; see Recipe 10.2 for more on this.

Discussion

Being able to identify an entity is the prerequisite for authentication and authorization. From the API server's point of view, there are two sorts of entities: human users and applications. While user identity (management) is outside of the scope of Kubernetes, there is a first-class resource representing the identity of an app: the service account.

Technically, the authentication of an app is captured by the token available in a file at the location /var/run/secrets/kubernetes.io/serviceaccount/token, which is mounted automatically through a secret. The service accounts are namespaced resources and are represented as follows:

```
system:serviceaccount:$NAMESPACE:$SERVICEACCOUNT
```

Listing the service accounts in a certain namespace gives you something like the following:

```
$ kubectl get sa
NAME          SECRETS   AGE
default       1         90d
myappsa       1         19m
prometheus    1         89d
```

Notice the service account called default here. This is created automatically; if you don't set the service account for a pod explicitly, as was done in the Solution, it will be assigned the default service account in its namespace.

See Also

- Managing Service Accounts (*https://kubernetes.io/docs/admin/service-accounts-admin/*)
- Configure Service Accounts for Pods (*https://kubernetes.io/docs/tasks/configure-pod-container/configure-service-account/*)
- Pull an Image from a Private Registry (*https://kubernetes.io/docs/tasks/configure-pod-container/pull-image-private-registry/*)

10.2 Listing and Viewing Access Control Information

Problem

You want to learn what actions you're allowed to do—for example, updating a deployment or listing secrets.

Solution

The following solution assumes you're using Role-Based Access Control as the authorization method (*https://kubernetes.io/docs/admin/authorization/*).

To check if a certain action on a resource is allowed for a specific user, use `kubectl auth can-i`. For example, you can execute this command to check if the service account `system:serviceaccount:sec:myappsa` is allowed to list pods in the namespace `sec`:

```
$ kubectl auth can-i list pods --as=system:serviceaccount:sec:myappsa -n=sec
yes
```

 If you want to try out this recipe in Minikube, you'll need to add `--extra-config=apiserver.Authorization.Mode=RBAC` when executing the binary.

To list the roles available in a namespace, do this:

```
$ kubectl get roles -n=kube-system
NAME                                                 AGE
extension-apiserver-authentication-reader            1d
system::leader-locking-kube-controller-manager       1d
system::leader-locking-kube-scheduler                1d
system:controller:bootstrap-signer                   1d
system:controller:cloud-provider                     1d
system:controller:token-cleaner                      1d

$ kubectl get clusterroles -n=kube-system
NAME                                                 AGE
admin                                                1d
cluster-admin                                        1d
edit                                                 1d
system:auth-delegator                                1d
system:basic-user                                    1d
system:controller:attachdetach-controller            1d
system:controller:certificate-controller             1d
system:controller:cronjob-controller                 1d
system:controller:daemon-set-controller              1d
system:controller:deployment-controller              1d
system:controller:disruption-controller              1d
system:controller:endpoint-controller                1d
system:controller:generic-garbage-collector          1d
system:controller:horizontal-pod-autoscaler          1d
system:controller:job-controller                     1d
system:controller:namespace-controller               1d
system:controller:node-controller                    1d
system:controller:persistent-volume-binder           1d
system:controller:pod-garbage-collector              1d
```

```
system:controller:replicaset-controller       1d
system:controller:replication-controller      1d
system:controller:resourcequota-controller    1d
system:controller:route-controller            1d
system:controller:service-account-controller  1d
system:controller:service-controller          1d
system:controller:statefulset-controller      1d
system:controller:ttl-controller              1d
system:discovery                               1d
system:heapster                                1d
system:kube-aggregator                         1d
system:kube-controller-manager                 1d
system:kube-dns                                1d
system:kube-scheduler                          1d
system:node                                    1d
system:node-bootstrapper                       1d
system:node-problem-detector                   1d
system:node-proxier                            1d
system:persistent-volume-provisioner           1d
view                                           1d
```

The output shows the predefined roles, which you can use directly for users and service accounts.

To further explore a certain role and understand what actions are allowed, use:

```
$ kubectl describe clusterroles/view -n=kube-system
Name:           view
Labels:         kubernetes.io/bootstrapping=rbac-defaults
Annotations:    rbac.authorization.kubernetes.io/autoupdate=true
PolicyRule:
  Resources                              Non-Resource URLs   ...  ...
  ---------                              -----------------   ---  ---
  bindings                               []                  ...  ...
  configmaps                             []                  ...  ...
  cronjobs.batch                         []                  ...  ...
  daemonsets.extensions                  []                  ...  ...
  deployments.apps                       []                  ...  ...
  deployments.extensions                 []                  ...  ...
  deployments.apps/scale                 []                  ...  ...
  deployments.extensions/scale           []                  ...  ...
  endpoints                              []                  ...  ...
  events                                 []                  ...  ...
  horizontalpodautoscalers.autoscaling   []                  ...  ...
  ingresses.extensions                   []                  ...  ...
  jobs.batch                             []                  ...  ...
  limitranges                            []                  ...  ...
  namespaces                             []                  ...  ...
  namespaces/status                      []                  ...  ...
  persistentvolumeclaims                 []                  ...  ...
  pods                                   []                  ...  ...
  pods/log                               []                  ...  ...
  pods/status                            []                  ...  ...
```

```
replicasets.extensions               []        ...  ...
replicasets.extensions/scale          []        ...  ...
replicationcontrollers                []        ...  ...
replicationcontrollers/scale          []        ...  ...
replicationcontrollers.extensions/scale  []     ...  ...
replicationcontrollers/status         []        ...  ...
resourcequotas                        []        ...  ...
resourcequotas/status                 []        ...  ...
scheduledjobs.batch                   []        ...  ...
serviceaccounts                       []        ...  ...
services                              []        ...  ...
statefulsets.apps                     []        ...  ...
```

In addition to the default roles defined in the kube-system namespace, you can define your own; see Recipe 10.3.

 When RBAC is enabled, in many environments (including Minikube and GKE) you might see a Forbidden (403) status code and an error message as shown below when you try to access the Kubernetes dashboard:

> User "system:serviceaccount:kube-system:default" cannot list pods in the namespace "sec". (get pods)

To access the dashboard, you'll need to give the kube-system:default service account the necessary rights:

```
$ kubectl create clusterrolebinding admin4kubesystem \
    --clusterrole=cluster-admin \
    --serviceaccount=kube-system:default
```

Note that this command gives the service account a lot of rights and might not be advisable in a production environment.

Discussion

As you can see in Figure 10-1, there are a couple of moving parts when dealing with RBAC authorization:

- An entity—that is, a group, user, or service account
- A resource, such as a pod, service, or secret
- A role, which defines rules for actions on a resource
- A role binding, which applies a role to an entity

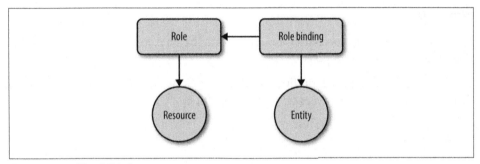

Figure 10-1. The RBAC concept

The actions on a resource that a role uses in its rules are the so-called verbs:

- `get, list, watch`
- `create`
- `update/patch`
- `delete`

Concerning the roles, we differentiate between two types:

- Cluster-wide: cluster roles and their respective cluster role bindings
- Namespace-wide: roles and role bindings

In Recipe 10.3, we will further discuss how you can create your own rules and apply them to users and resources.

See Also

- Kubernetes Authorization Overview (*https://kubernetes.io/docs/admin/authoriza tion/*)
- Using RBAC Authorization (*https://kubernetes.io/docs/admin/authorization/ rbac/*)

10.3 Controlling Access to Resources

Problem

For a given user or application, you want to allow or deny a certain action, such as viewing secrets or updating a deployment.

Solution

Let's assume you want to restrict an app to only be able to view pods—that is, list pods and get details about pods.

You'd start off with a pod definition in a YAML manifest, *pod-with-sa.yaml*, using a dedicated service account, myappsa (see Recipe 10.1):

```
kind:               Pod
apiVersion:         v1
metadata:
  name:             myapp
  namespace:        sec
spec:
  serviceAccountName: myappsa
  containers:
  - name:           main
    image:          centos:7
    command:
      - "bin/bash"
      - "-c"
      - "sleep 10000"
```

Next, you'd define a role—let's call it podreader in the manifest *pod-reader.yaml*—that defines the allowed actions on resources:

```
kind:          Role
apiVersion:    rbac.authorization.k8s.io/v1beta1
metadata:
  name:        podreader
  namespace: sec
rules:
- apiGroups: [""]
  resources: ["pods"]
  verbs:       ["get", "list"]
```

Last but not least you need to apply the role podreader to the service account myappsa, using a role binding in *pod-reader-binding.yaml*:

```
kind:          RoleBinding
apiVersion:    rbac.authorization.k8s.io/v1beta1
metadata:
  name:        podreaderbinding
  namespace: sec
roleRef:
  apiGroup:    rbac.authorization.k8s.io
  kind:        Role
  name:        podreader
subjects:
- kind:        ServiceAccount
  name:        myappsa
  namespace: sec
```

When creating the respective resources, you can use the YAML manifests directly (assuming the service account has already been created):

```
$ kubectl create -f pod-reader.yaml
$ kubectl create -f pod-reader-binding.yaml
$ kubectl create -f pod-with-sa.yaml
```

Rather than creating manifests for the role and the role binding, you can use the following commands:

```
$ kubectl create role podreader \
          --verb=get --verb=list \
          --resource=pods -n=sec

$ kubectl create rolebinding podreaderbinding \
          --role=sec:podreader \
          --serviceaccount=sec:myappsa \
          --namespace=sec -n=sec
```

Note that this is a case of namespaced access control setup, since you're using roles and role bindings. For cluster-wide access control, you'd use the corresponding `create clusterrole` and `create clusterrolebinding` commands.

Sometimes it's not obvious if you should use a role or a cluster role and/or role binding, so here are a few rules of thumb you might find useful:

- If you want to restrict access to a namespaced resource (like a service or pod) in a certain namespace, use a role and a role binding (as we did in this recipe).

- If you want to reuse a role in a couple of namespaces, use a cluster role with a role binding.

- If you want to restrict access to cluster-wide resources such as nodes or to namespaced resources across all namespaces, use a cluster role with a cluster role binding.

See Also

- Configure RBAC in Your Kubernetes Cluster (*https://docs.bitnami.com/kuber netes/how-to/configure-rbac-in-your-kubernetes-cluster/*)

- Antoine Cotten's blog post "Kubernetes v1.7 Security in Practice" (*https://acot ten.com/post/kube17-security*)

10.4 Securing Pods

Problem

You want to define the security context for an app on the pod level. For example, you want to run the app as a nonprivileged process or restrict the types of volumes the app can access.

Solution

To enforce policies on the pod level in Kubernetes, use the securityContext field in a pod specification.

Let's assume you want an app running as a nonroot user. For this, you'd use the security context on the container level as shown in the following manifest, *secured-pod.yaml*:

```
kind:           Pod
apiVersion:     v1
metadata:
  name:         secpod
spec:
  containers:
  - name:       shell
    image:      centos:7
    command:
      - "bin/bash"
      - "-c"
      - "sleep 10000"
    securityContext:
      runAsUser:    5000
```

Now create the pod and check the user under which the container runs:

```
$ kubectl create -f securedpod.yaml
pod "secpod" created

$ kubectl exec secpod ps aux
USER      PID %CPU %MEM    VSZ   RSS TTY     STAT START   TIME COMMAND
5000        1  0.0  0.0   4328   672 ?       Ss   12:39   0:00 sleep 10000
5000        8  0.0  0.1  47460  3108 ?       Rs   12:40   0:00 ps aux
```

As expected, it's running as the user with ID 5000. Note that you can also use the securityContext field on the pod level rather than on specific containers.

A more powerful method to enforce policies on the pod level is to use pod security policies (PSP). These are cluster-wide resources that allows you to define a range of policies, including some similar to what you've seen here but also restrictions around storage and networking. For a walk-through on how to use PSPs, see "Secure a

Kubernetes Cluster with Pod Security Policies" (*https://docs.bitnami.com/kubernetes/how-to/secure-kubernetes-cluster-psp/*) in the Bitnami docs for Kubernetes.

See Also

- Pod Security Policies documentation (*https://kubernetes.io/docs/concepts/policy/pod-security-policy/*)
- Configure a Security Context for a Pod or Container (*https://kubernetes.io/docs/tasks/configure-pod-container/security-context/*)

## CHAPTER 11

Monitoring and Logging

In this chapter, we focus on recipes around monitoring and logging, both on the infrastructure and on the application level. In the context of Kubernetes, different roles typically have different scopes:

- *Administrator roles*, such as cluster admins, networking operations folks, or namespace-level admins, focus on infrastructure aspects. Exemplary questions might be: Are nodes healthy? Shall we add a worker node? What is the cluster-wide utilization? Are users close to their usage quotas?

- *Developer roles* mainly think and act in the context of their applications, which may well be—in the age of microservices—a handful to a dozen. For example, a person in a developer role might ask: Do I have enough resources allocated to run my app? How many replicas should I scale my app to? Do I have access to the right volumes, and how full are they? Is one of my apps failing and, if so, why?

We will first discuss recipes around cluster-internal monitoring leveraging Kubernetes liveness and readiness probes, then focus on monitoring with Heapster (*https://github.com/kubernetes/heapster*) and Prometheus (*https://prometheus.io/*), and finally cover logging-related recipes.

11.1 Accessing the Logs of a Container

Problem

You want to access the logs of the application running inside a container that is running in a specific pod.

Solution

Use the `kubectl logs` command. To see the various options, check the usage, like so:

```
$ kubectl logs --help | more
Print the logs for a container in a pod or specified resource. If the pod has only
one container, the container name is optional.

Aliases:
logs, log

Examples:
  # Return snapshot logs from pod nginx with only one container
  kubectl logs nginx
...
```

For example, given a pod started by a deployment (see Recipe 4.1), you can check the logs like so:

```
$ kubectl get pods
NAME                       READY    STATUS     RESTARTS   AGE
ghost-8449997474-kn86m     1/1      Running    0          1m

$ kubectl logs ghost-8449997474-kn86m
[2017-12-16 18:44:18] INFO Creating table: posts
[2017-12-16 18:44:18] INFO Creating table: users
[2017-12-16 18:44:18] INFO Creating table: roles
[2017-12-16 18:44:18] INFO Creating table: roles_users
...
```

 If a pod has multiple containers, you can get the logs of any of them by specifying the name of the container using the -c option of kubectl logs.

11.2 Recover from a Broken State with a Liveness Probe

Problem

You want to make sure that if the applications running inside some of your pods get into a broken state, Kubernetes restarts the pods automatically.

Solution

Use a liveness probe.[1] If the probe fails, the `kubelet` will restart the pod automatically. The probe is part of the pod specification and is added to the `containers` section. Each container in a pod can have a liveness probe.

A probe can be of three different types: it can be a command that is executed inside the container, an HTTP request to a specific route served by a web server inside the container, or a more generic TCP probe.

In the following example, we show a basic HTTP probe:

```
apiVersion:  v1
kind:        Pod
metadata:
  name:      liveness-nginx
spec:
  containers:
  - name:      liveness
    image:     nginx
    livenessProbe:
      httpGet:
        path: /
        port: 80
```

See Recipe 11.4 for a complete example.

See Also

- Kubernetes Container probes documentation (*https://kubernetes.io/docs/concepts/workloads/pods/pod-lifecycle/#container-probes*).

11.3 Controlling Traffic Flow to a Pod Using a Readiness Probe

Problem

Your pods are up and running according to the liveness probes (see Recipe 11.2), but you only want to send traffic to them if the application is ready to serve the requests.

---

1 Kubernetes, "Configure Liveness and Readiness Probes" (*https://kubernetes.io/docs/tasks/configure-pod-container/configure-liveness-readiness-probes/#define-a-liveness-command*).

Solution

Add readiness probes to your pod specifications.[2] Similar to liveness probes, readiness probes can be of three types (see the documentation for details). The following is a straightforward example of running a single pod with the `nginx` Docker image. The readiness probe makes an HTTP request to port 80:

```
apiVersion:   v1
kind:         Pod
metadata:
  name:       readiness-nginx
spec:
  containers:
  - name:       readiness
    image:      nginx
    readinessProbe:
      httpGet:
        path:  /
        port:  80
```

Discussion

While the readiness probe shown in this recipe is the same as the liveness probe in Recipe 11.2, they typically should be different as the two probes aim to give information about different aspects of the application. The liveness probe checks to see that the application process is alive, but it may not be ready to accept requests. The readiness probe checks that the application is serving requests properly. As such, only when a readiness probe passes does the pod become part of a service (see Recipe 5.1).

See Also

- Kubernetes Container probes documentation (*https://kubernetes.io/docs/concepts/workloads/pods/pod-lifecycle/#container-probes*)

11.4 Adding Liveness and Readiness Probes to Your Deployments

Problem

You want to be able to automatically check if your app is healthy and let Kubernetes take action if this is not the case.

---

2 Kubernetes, "Define readiness probes" (*https://kubernetes.io/docs/tasks/configure-pod-container/configure-liveness-readiness-probes/#define-readiness-probes*).

Solution

To signal to Kubernetes how your app is doing, add liveness and readiness probes as described here.

The starting point is a deployment manifest, *webserver.yaml*:

```
apiVersion:          extensions/v1beta1
kind:                Deployment
metadata:
  name:              webserver
spec:
  replicas:          1
  template:
    metadata:
      labels:
        app:         nginx
    spec:
      containers:
      - name:        nginx
        image:       nginx:stable
        ports:
        - containerPort: 80
```

Liveness and readiness probes are defined in the containers section of the pod specification. See the introductory examples (Recipe 11.2 and Recipe 11.3) and add the following to your container spec in your deployment's pod template:

```
...
    livenessProbe:
      initialDelaySecond: 2
      periodSeconds: 10
      httpGet:
        path: /
        port: 80
    readinessProbe:
      initialDelaySecond: 2
      periodSeconds: 10
      httpGet:
        path: /
        port: 80
...
```

And now you can launch it and check the probes:

```
$ kubectl create -f webserver.yaml

$ kubectl get pods
NAME                          READY   STATUS    RESTARTS   AGE
webserver-4288715076-dk9c7    1/1     Running   0          2m

$ kubectl describe pod/webserver-4288715076-dk9c7
Name:           webserver-4288715076-dk9c7
```

```
Namespace:       default
Node:            node/172.17.0.128
...
Status:          Running
IP:              10.32.0.2
Controllers:     ReplicaSet/webserver-4288715076
Containers:
  nginx:
    ...
    Ready:          True
    Restart Count:  0
    Liveness:       http-get http://:80/ delay=2s timeout=1s period=10s #...
...
```

Note that the output of the kubectl describe command has been edited down to the important bits; there's much more information available but it's not pertinent to our problem here.

Discussion

In order to verify if a container in a pod is healthy and ready to serve traffic, Kubernetes provides a range of health-checking mechanisms. Health checks, or *probes* as they are called in Kubernetes, are defined on the container level, not on the pod level, and are carried out by two different components:

- The kubelet on each worker node uses the livenessProbe directive in the spec to determine when to restart a container. These liveness probes can help overcome ramp-up issues or deadlocks.

- A service load balancing a set of pods uses the readinessProbe directive to determine if a pod is ready and hence should receive traffic. If this is not the case, it is excluded from the service's pool of endpoints. Note that a pod is considered ready when all of its containers are ready.

When should you use which probe? That depends on the behavior of the container, really. Use a liveness probe and a restartPolicy of either Always or OnFailure if your container can and should be killed and restarted if the probe fails. If you want to send traffic to a pod only when it's ready, use a readiness probe. Note that in this latter case, the readiness probe can be the same as the liveness probe.

See Also

- Configure Liveness and Readiness Probes (*https://kubernetes.io/docs/tasks/configure-pod-container/configure-liveness-readiness-probes/*)

- Pod Lifecycle documentation (*https://kubernetes.io/docs/concepts/workloads/pods/pod-lifecycle/*)

- Init Containers documentation (*https://kubernetes.io/docs/concepts/workloads/ pods/init-containers/*) (stable in v1.6 and above)

11.5 Enabling Heapster on Minikube to Monitor Resources

Problem

You want to use the `kubectl top` command in Minikube to monitor resource usage, but it appears that the Heapster add-on is not running:

```
$ kubectl top pods
Error from server (NotFound): the server could not find the requested resource
(get services http:heapster:)
```

Solution

The latest versions of the `minikube` command include an add-on manager, which lets you enable Heapster—as well as a few other add-ons, such as an ingress controller—with a single command:

```
$ minikube addons enable heapster
```

Enabling the Heapster add-on triggers the creation of two pods in the `kube-system` namespace: one pod running Heapster and another pod running an InfluxDB (*https://www.influxdata.com/*) time-series database along with a Grafana (*https:// grafana.com/grafana*) dashboard.

After some minutes, once the first metrics have been collected, the `kubectl top` command will return resource metrics as expected:

```
$ kubectl top node
NAME       CPU(cores)   CPU%   MEMORY(bytes)   MEMORY%
minikube   187m         9%     1154Mi          60%

$ kubectl top pods --all-namespaces
NAMESPACE     NAME                            CPU(cores)   MEMORY(bytes)
default       ghost-2663835528-fb044          0m           140Mi
kube-system   kube-dns-v20-4bkhn              3m           12Mi
kube-system   heapster-6j5m8                  0m           21Mi
kube-system   influxdb-grafana-vw9x1          23m          37Mi
kube-system   kube-addon-manager-minikube     47m          3Mi
kube-system   kubernetes-dashboard-scsnx      0m           14Mi
kube-system   default-http-backend-75m71      0m           1Mi
kube-system   nginx-ingress-controller-p8fmd  4m           51Mi
```

Now you will also be able to access the Grafana dashboard and customize it to your liking:

```
$ minikube service monitoring-grafana -n kube-system
Waiting, endpoint for service is not ready yet...
Waiting, endpoint for service is not ready yet...
Waiting, endpoint for service is not ready yet...
Waiting, endpoint for service is not ready yet...
Opening kubernetes service kube-system/monitoring-grafana in default browser...
```

As a result of this command, your default browser should automagically open and you should see something like Figure 11-1.

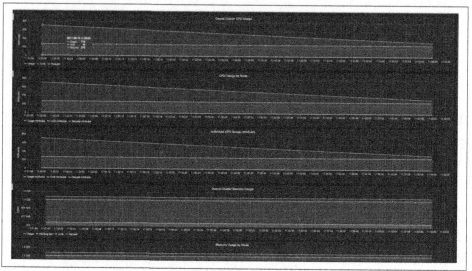

Figure 11-1. Screenshot of the Grafana dashboard, showing Minikube metrics

Note that you can drill into the metrics in Grafana at this point.

11.6 Using Prometheus on Minikube

Problem

You want to view and query the system and application metrics of your cluster in a central place.

Solution

Use Prometheus as follows:

1. Create a config map holding the Prometheus configuration.

2. Set up a service account for Prometheus and assign permissions via RBAC (see Recipe 10.3) to the service account (see Recipe 10.1) allowing access to all metrics.

3. Create an app consisting of a deployment, a service, and an `Ingress` resource for Prometheus so that you can access it via a browser from outside the cluster.

First, you need to set up the Prometheus configuration via a `ConfigMap` object (see Recipe 8.3 for an introduction to config maps). You will be using this later in the Prometheus app. Create a file called *prometheus.yml*, holding the Prometheus configuration, with the following content:

```
global:
  scrape_interval:        5s
  evaluation_interval:    5s
scrape_configs:
- job_name:               'kubernetes-nodes'
  scheme:                 https
  tls_config:
    ca_file:              /var/run/secrets/kubernetes.io/serviceaccount/ca.crt
    server_name:          'gke-k8scb-default-pool-be16f9ee-522p'
    insecure_skip_verify: true
  bearer_token_file:      /var/run/secrets/kubernetes.io/serviceaccount/token
  kubernetes_sd_configs:
  - role:                 node
  relabel_configs:
  - action:               labelmap
    regex:                __meta_kubernetes_node_label_(.+)
- job_name:               'kubernetes-cadvisor'
  scheme:                 https
  tls_config:
    ca_file:              /var/run/secrets/kubernetes.io/serviceaccount/ca.crt
  bearer_token_file:      /var/run/secrets/kubernetes.io/serviceaccount/token
  kubernetes_sd_configs:
  - role:                 node
  relabel_configs:
  - action:               labelmap
    regex:                __meta_kubernetes_node_label_(.+)
  - target_label:         __address__
    replacement:          kubernetes.default.svc:443
  - source_labels:        [__meta_kubernetes_node_name]
    regex:                (.+)
    target_label:         __metrics_path__
    replacement:          /api/v1/nodes/${1}:4194/proxy/metrics
```

We can use this to create a config map, like so:

```
$ kubectl create configmap prom-config-cm --from-file=prometheus.yml
```

Next, set up the Prometheus service account and role binding (permissions) in a manifest file called *prometheus-rbac.yaml*, as follows:

```
apiVersion: v1
kind:       ServiceAccount
metadata:
  name:     prometheus
```

```
  namespace: default
---
apiVersion:  rbac.authorization.k8s.io/v1beta1
kind:        ClusterRoleBinding
metadata:
  name:      prometheus
roleRef:
  apiGroup:  rbac.authorization.k8s.io
  kind:      ClusterRole
  name:      cluster-admin
subjects:
- kind:      ServiceAccount
  name:      prometheus
  namespace: default
```

Using this manifest, you can now create the service account and role binding:

```
$ kubectl create -f prometheus-rbac.yaml
```

Now that you have all the prerequisites sorted (configuration and access permissions), you can move on to the Prometheus app itself. Remember, the app consists of a deployment, a service, and an `Ingress` resource and uses the config map and service account you created in the previous steps.

Next, define the Prometheus app manifest in *prometheus-app.yaml*:

```
kind:                         Deployment
apiVersion:                   extensions/v1beta1
metadata:
  name:                       prom
  namespace:                  default
  labels:
    app:                      prom
spec:
  replicas:                   1
  selector:
    matchLabels:
      app:                    prom
  template:
    metadata:
      name:                   prom
      labels:
        app:                  prom
    spec:
      serviceAccount:         prometheus
      containers:
      - name:                 prom
        image:                prom/prometheus
        imagePullPolicy:      Always
        volumeMounts:
        - name:               prometheus-volume-1
          mountPath:          "/prometheus"
        - name:               prom-config-volume
```

```yaml
          mountPath:                       "/etc/prometheus/"
       volumes:
       - name:                             prometheus-volume-1
         emptyDir:                         {}
       - name:                             prom-config-volume
         configMap:
           name:                           prom-config-cm
           defaultMode:                    420
---
kind:                                      Service
apiVersion:                                v1
metadata:
  name:                                    prom-svc
  labels:
    app:                                   prom
spec:
  ports:
  - port:                                  80
    targetPort:                            9090
  selector:
    app:                                   prom
  type:                                    LoadBalancer
  externalTrafficPolicy:                   Cluster
---
kind:                                      Ingress
apiVersion:                                extensions/v1beta1
metadata:
  name:                                    prom-public
  annotations:
    ingress.kubernetes.io/rewrite-target:  /
spec:
  rules:
  - host:
    http:
      paths:
      - path:                              /
        backend:
          serviceName:                     prom-svc
          servicePort:                     80
```

And now create the app from the manifest:

```
$ kubectl create -f prometheus-app.yaml
```

Congratulations—you just created a full-fledged app! Now you can access Prometheus via $MINISHIFT_IP/graph (for example, https://192.168.99.100/graph), and you should see something like in Figure 11-2.

Figure 11-2. Prometheus screenshot

Discussion

Prometheus is a powerful and flexible monitoring and alerting system. You can use it —or better, one of the many instrumentation libraries (*https://prometheus.io/docs/ instrumenting/clientlibs/*)—to make your own app report higher-level metrics such as, the number of transactions performed, just like the way, say, a kubelet reports the CPU usage.

While Prometheus is fast and scalable, you probable want to use something else to visualize the metrics. The canonical way to do this is to connect it with Grafana (*https://prometheus.io/docs/visualization/grafana/*).

There is a known issue (*https://github.com/prometheus/prometheus/ issues/2916*) with using Prometheus with Kubernetes versions 1.7.0 through 1.7.2, as the kubelet's behavior concerning exposing con‐ tainer metrics changed in v1.7.0.

Note that the Prometheus config shown in the Solution is valid for v1.7.0 to v1.7.2; if you're using v1.7.3 or later, you want to check out the example Prometheus configuration file (*https://github.com/ prometheus/prometheus/blob/master/documentation/examples/ prometheus-kubernetes.yml#L88*) for details on what you need to change.

Note that the solution described here is not limited to Minikube. In fact, as long as you can create the service account (that is, you have sufficient rights to give Prometheus the necessary permissions), you can apply the same solution to environments such as GKE, ACS, or OpenShift.

See Also

- Instrumentation in the Prometheus docs (*https://prometheus.io/docs/practices/instrumentation/*)

- Grafana with Prometheus in the Prometheus docs (*https://prometheus.io/docs/visualization/grafana/*)

11.7 Using Elasticsearch–Fluentd–Kibana (EFK) on Minikube

Problem

You want to view and query the logs of all of the apps in your cluster in a central place.

Solution

Use Elasticsearch, Fluentd (*https://www.fluentd.org/*), and Kibana (*https://www.elastic.co/products/kibana*) as described here.

As preparation, make sure Minikube has enough resources assigned. For example, use `--cpus=4 --memory=4000` and make sure the ingress add-on is enabled, like so:

```
$ minikube start
Starting local Kubernetes v1.7.0 cluster...
Starting VM...
Getting VM IP address...
Moving files into cluster...
Setting up certs...
Starting cluster components...
Connecting to cluster...
Setting up kubeconfig...
Kubectl is now configured to use the cluster.

$ minikube addons list | grep ingress
- ingress: enabled
```

If the add-on is not enabled, enable it:

```
$ minikube addons enable ingress
```

Next, create a manifest file called *efk-logging.yaml* with the following content:

```
kind:                                     Ingress
apiVersion:                               extensions/v1beta1
metadata:
  name:                                   kibana-public
  annotations:
    ingress.kubernetes.io/rewrite-target: /
spec:
  rules:
  - host:
    http:
      paths:
      - path:                             /
        backend:
          serviceName:                    kibana
          servicePort:                    5601
---
kind:                                     Service
apiVersion:                               v1
metadata:
  labels:
    app:                                  efk
  name:                                   kibana
spec:
  ports:
  - port:                                 5601
  selector:
    app:                                  efk
---
kind:                                     Deployment
apiVersion:                               extensions/v1beta1
metadata:
  name:                                   kibana
spec:
  replicas:                               1
  template:
    metadata:
      labels:
        app:                              efk
    spec:
      containers:
      - env:
        - name:                           ELASTICSEARCH_URL
          value:                          http://elasticsearch:9200
        name:                             kibana
        image:                            docker.elastic.co/kibana/kibana:5.5.1
        ports:
          - containerPort:                5601
---
kind:                                     Service
apiVersion:                               v1
metadata:
```

```yaml
    labels:
      app:                  efk
    name:                   elasticsearch
spec:
  ports:
  - port:                   9200
  selector:
    app:                    efk
---
kind:                       Deployment
apiVersion:                 extensions/v1beta1
metadata:
  name:                     es
spec:
  replicas:                 1
  template:
    metadata:
      labels:
        app:                efk
    spec:
      containers:
      - name:               es
        image:              docker.elastic.co/elasticsearch/
                            elasticsearch:5.5.1
        ports:
        - containerPort:    9200
        env:
        - name:             ES_JAVA_OPTS
          value:            "-Xms256m -Xmx256m"
---
kind:                       DaemonSet
apiVersion:                 extensions/v1beta1
metadata:
  name:                     fluentd
spec:
  template:
    metadata:
      labels:
        app:                efk
        name:               fluentd
    spec:
      containers:
      - name:               fluentd
        image:              gcr.io/google_containers/fluentd-
                            elasticsearch:1.3
        env:
        - name:             FLUENTD_ARGS
          value:            -qq
        volumeMounts:
        - name:             varlog
          mountPath:        /varlog
        - name:             containers
```

```
         mountPath:                        /var/lib/docker/containers
    volumes:
       - hostPath:
           path:                           /var/log
         name:                             varlog
       - hostPath:
           path:                           /var/lib/docker/containers
         name:                             containers
```

Now you can launch the EFK stack:

```
$ kubectl create -f efk-logging.yaml
```

Once everything has started up, log in to Kibana with the following credentials:

- Username: kibana

- Password: changeme

Visit the Discover tab at https://$IP/app/kibana#/discover?_g=() and start exploring the logs from there.

If you want to clean up and/or restart the EFK stack, use the following:

```
$ kubectl delete deploy/es && \
  kubectl delete deploy/kibana && \
  kubectl delete svc/elasticsearch && \
  kubectl delete svc/kibana && \
  kubectl delete ingress/kibana-public && \
  kubectl delete daemonset/fluentd
```

Discussion

The log shipping can also be done using Logstash. We chose to use Fluentd in the Solution because it's a CNCF project and is gaining a lot of traction.

Note that Kibana can take some time to come up, and you might need to reload the web app a couple of times before you get to the configuration bits.

See Also

- Manoj Bhagwat's blog post "To Centralize Your Docker Logs with Fluentd and ElasticSearch on Kubernetes" (*https://medium.com/@manoj.bhagwat60/to-centralize-your-docker-logs-with-fluentd-and-elasticsearch-on-kubernetes-42d2ac0e8b6c*)

- Kubernetes EFK Stack for AWS (*https://github.com/Skillshare/kubernetes-efk*)

- elk-kubernetes (*https://github.com/kayrus/elk-kubernetes*)

## CHAPTER 12

Maintenance and Troubleshooting

In this chapter, you will find recipes that deal with both app-level and cluster-level maintenance. We cover various aspects of troubleshooting, from debugging pods and containers, to testing service connectivity, interpreting a resource's status, and node maintenance. Last but not least, we look at how to deal with etcd, the Kubernetes control plane storage component. This chapter is relevant for both cluster admins and app developers.

12.1 Enabling Autocomplete for kubectl

Problem

It is cumbersome to type full commands and arguments for the kubectl command, so you want an autocomplete function for it.

Solution

Enable autocompletion for kubectl.

For Linux and the *bash* shell, you can enable kubectl autocompletion in your current shell using the following command:

```
$ source <(kubectl completion bash)
```

For other operating systems and shells, please check the documentation (*https://kuber netes.io/docs/tasks/tools/install-kubectl/#enabling-shell-autocompletion*).

See Also

- Overview of kubectl (*https://kubernetes.io/docs/user-guide/kubectl-overview/*)
- kubectl Cheat Sheet (*https://kubernetes.io/docs/user-guide/kubectl-cheatsheet/*)

12.2 Removing a Pod from a Service

Problem

You have a well-defined service (see Recipe 5.1) backed by several pods. But one of the pods is misbehaving, and you would like to take it out of the list of endpoints to examine it at a later time.

Solution

Relabel the pod using the `--overwrite` option—this will allow you to change the value of the `run` label on the pod. By overwriting this label, you can ensure that it will not be selected by the service selector (Recipe 5.1) and will be removed from the list of endpoints. At the same time, the replica set watching over your pods will see that a pod has disappeared and will start a new replica.

To see this in action, start with a straightforward deployment generated with `kubectl run` (see Recipe 4.4):

```
$ kubectl run nginx --image nginx --replicas 4
```

When you list the pods and show the label with key `run`, you'll see four pods with the value `nginx` (`run=nginx` is the label that is automatically generated by the `kubectl run` command):

```
$ kubectl get pods -Lrun
NAME                       READY     STATUS      RESTARTS   AGE    RUN
nginx-d5dc44cf7-5g45r      1/1       Running     0          1h     nginx
nginx-d5dc44cf7-l429b      1/1       Running     0          1h     nginx
nginx-d5dc44cf7-pvrfh      1/1       Running     0          1h     nginx
nginx-d5dc44cf7-vm764      1/1       Running     0          1h     nginx
```

You can then expose this deployment with a service and check the endpoints, which correspond to the IP addresses of each pod:

```
$ kubectl expose deployments nginx --port 80

$ kubectl get endpoints
NAME       ENDPOINTS                                               AGE
nginx      172.17.0.11:80,172.17.0.14:80,172.17.0.3:80 + 1 more...  1h
```

Moving the first pod out of the service traffic via relabeling is done with a single command:

```
$ kubectl label pods nginx-d5dc44cf7-5g45r run=notworking --overwrite
```

 To find the IP address of a pod, you can list the pod's manifest in JSON and run a JQuery query:

```
$ kubectl get pods nginx-d5dc44cf7-5g45r -o json | \
  jq -r .status.podIP172.17.0.3
```

You will see a brand new pod appear with the label run=nginx, and you will see that your nonworking pod still exists but no longer appears in the list of service endpoints:

```
$ kubectl get pods -Lrun
NAME                      READY   STATUS    RESTARTS   AGE   RUN
nginx-d5dc44cf7-5g45r     1/1     Running   0          21h   notworking
nginx-d5dc44cf7-hztlw     1/1     Running   0          21s   nginx
nginx-d5dc44cf7-l429b     1/1     Running   0          5m    nginx
nginx-d5dc44cf7-pvrfh     1/1     Running   0          5m    nginx
nginx-d5dc44cf7-vm764     1/1     Running   0          5m    nginx

$ kubectl describe endpoints nginx
Name:          nginx
Namespace:     default
Labels:        run=nginx
Annotations:   <none>
Subsets:
  Addresses:            172.17.0.11,172.17.0.14,172.17.0.19,172.17.0.7
...
```

12.3 Accessing a ClusterIP Service Outside the Cluster

Problem

You have an internal service that is causing you trouble and you want to test that it is working well locally without exposing the service externally.

Solution

Use a local proxy to the Kubernetes API server with kubectl proxy.

Let's assume that you have created a deployment and a service as described in Recipe 12.2. You should see an nginx service when you list the services:

```
$ kubectl get svc
NAME     TYPE        CLUSTER-IP     EXTERNAL-IP   PORT(S)   AGE
nginx    ClusterIP   10.109.24.56   <none>        80/TCP    22h
```

This service is not reachable outside the Kubernetes cluster. However, you can run a proxy in a separate terminal and then reach it on `localhost`.

Start by running the proxy in a separate terminal:

```
$ kubectl proxy
Starting to serve on 127.0.0.1:8001
```

You can specify the port that you want the proxy to run on with the `--port` option.

In your original terminal, you can then use your browser or `curl` to access the application exposed by your service. Note the specific path to the service; it contains a `/proxy` part. Without this, you get the JSON object representing the service:

```
$ curl http://localhost:8001/api/v1/proxy/namespaces/default/services/nginx/
<!DOCTYPE html>
<html>
<head>
<title>Welcome to nginx!</title>
...
```

Note that you can now also access the entire Kubernetes API over `localhost` using `curl`.

12.4 Understanding and Parsing Resource Statuses

Problem

You want to react based on the status of a resource—say, a pod—in a script or in another automated environment like a CI/CD pipeline.

Solution

Use `kubectl get $KIND/$NAME -o json` and parse the JSON output using one of the two methods described here.

If you have the JSON query utility jq installed (*https://github.com/stedolan/jq/wiki/Installation*), you can use it to parse the resource status. Let's assume you have a pod called jump and want to know what Quality of Service (QoS) class[1] the pod is in:

```
$ kubectl get po/jump -o json | jq --raw-output .status.qosClass
BestEffort
```

Note that the --raw-output argument for jq will show the raw value and that .status.qosClass is the expression that matches the respective subfield.

Another status query could be around the events or state transitions:

```
$ kubectl get po/jump -o json | jq .status.conditions
[
  {
    "lastProbeTime": null,
    "lastTransitionTime": "2017-08-28T08:06:19Z",
    "status": "True",
    "type": "Initialized"
  },
  {
    "lastProbeTime": null,
    "lastTransitionTime": "2017-08-31T08:21:29Z",
    "status": "True",
    "type": "Ready"
  },
  {
    "lastProbeTime": null,
    "lastTransitionTime": "2017-08-28T08:06:19Z",
    "status": "True",
    "type": "PodScheduled"
  }
]
```

Of course, these queries are not limited to pods—you can apply this technique to any resource. For example, you can query the revisions of a deployment:

```
$ kubectl get deploy/prom -o json | jq .metadata.annotations
{
  "deployment.kubernetes.io/revision": "1"
}
```

Or you can list all the endpoints that make up a service:

```
$ kubectl get ep/prom-svc -o json | jq '.subsets'
[
  {
    "addresses": [
      {
```

---

1 Medium, "What are Quality of Service (QoS) Classes in Kubernetes" (*https://medium.com/google-cloud/quality-of-service-class-qos-in-kubernetes-bb76a89eb2c6*).

```
        "ip": "172.17.0.4",
        "nodeName": "minikube",
        "targetRef": {
          "kind": "Pod",
          "name": "prom-2436944326-pr60g",
          "namespace": "default",
          "resourceVersion": "686093",
          "uid": "eee59623-7f2f-11e7-b58a-080027390640"
        }
      }
    ],
    "ports": [
      {
        "port": 9090,
        "protocol": "TCP"
      }
    ]
  }
]
```

Now that you've seen jq in action, let's move on to a method that doesn't require external tooling—that is, the built-in feature of using Go templates.

The Go programming language defines templates in a package called text/template that can be used for any kind of text or data transformation, and kubectl has built-in support for it. For example, to list all the container images used in the current namespace, do this:

```
$ kubectl get pods -o go-template \
        --template="{{range .items}}{{range .spec.containers}}{{.image}} \
        {{end}}{{end}}"
busybox prom/prometheus
```

See Also

- jq Manual (*https://stedolan.github.io/jq/manual/*)

- jq playground (*https://jqplay.org/*) to try out queries without installing jq

- Package Template in the Go docs (*https://golang.org/pkg/text/template/*)

12.5 Debugging Pods

Problem

You have a situation where a pod is either not starting up as expected or fails after some time.

Solution

To systematically discover and fix the cause of the problem, enter an OODA loop (*https://en.wikipedia.org/wiki/OODA_loop*):

1. *Observe.* What do you see in the container logs? What events have occurred? How is the network connectivity?

2. *Orient.* Formulate a set of plausible hypotheses—stay as open-minded as possible and don't jump to conclusions.

3. *Decide.* Pick one of the hypotheses.

4. *Act.* Test the hypothesis. If it's confirmed, you're done; otherwise, go back to step 1 and continue.

Let's have a look at a concrete example where a pod fails. Create a manifest called *unhappy-pod.yaml* with this content:

```
apiVersion:        extensions/v1beta1
kind:              Deployment
metadata:
  name:            unhappy
spec:
  replicas:        1
  template:
    metadata:
      labels:
        app:       nevermind
    spec:
      containers:
      - name:      shell
        image:     busybox
        command:
        - "sh"
        - "-c"
        - "echo I will just print something here and then exit"
```

Now when you launch that deployment and look at the pod it creates, you'll see it's unhappy:

```
$ kubectl create -f unhappy-pod.yaml
deployment "unhappy" created

$ kubectl  get po
NAME                        READY    STATUS             RESTARTS   AGE
unhappy-3626010456-4j251    0/1      CrashLoopBackOff   1          7s

$ kubectl describe po/unhappy-3626010456-4j251
Name:           unhappy-3626010456-4j251
Namespace:      default
Node:           minikube/192.168.99.100
```

```
Start Time:       Sat, 12 Aug 2017 17:02:37 +0100
Labels:           app=nevermind
                  pod-template-hash=3626010456
Annotations:      kubernetes.io/created-by={"kind":"SerializedReference","apiVersion":
"v1","reference":{"kind":"ReplicaSet","namespace":"default","name":
"unhappy-3626010456","uid":
"a9368a97-7f77-11e7-b58a-080027390640"...
Status:           Running
IP:               172.17.0.13
Created By:       ReplicaSet/unhappy-3626010456
Controlled By:    ReplicaSet/unhappy-3626010456
...
Conditions:
  Type            Status
  Initialized     True
  Ready           False
  PodScheduled    True
Volumes:
  default-token-rlm2s:
    Type:         Secret (a volume populated by a Secret)
    SecretName:   default-token-rlm2s
    Optional:     false
QoS Class:        BestEffort
Node-Selectors:   <none>
Tolerations:      <none>
Events:
  FirstSeen   ...   Reason                Message
  ---------   ...   ------                -------
  25s         ...   Scheduled             Successfully assigned
                                          unhappy-3626010456-4j251 to minikube
  25s         ...   SuccessfulMountVolume MountVolume.SetUp succeeded for
                                          volume "default-token-rlm2s"
  24s         ...   Pulling               pulling image "busybox"
  22s         ...   Pulled                Successfully pulled image "busybox"
  22s         ...   Created               Created container
  22s         ...   Started               Started container
  19s         ...   BackOff               Back-off restarting failed container
  19s         ...   FailedSync            Error syncing pod
```

As you can see, Kubernetes considers this pod as not ready to serve traffic as it encountered an "error syncing pod."

Another way to observe this is using the Kubernetes dashboard to view the deployment (Figure 12-1), as well as the supervised replica set and the pod (Figure 12-2).

Figure 12-1. Screenshot of deployment in error state

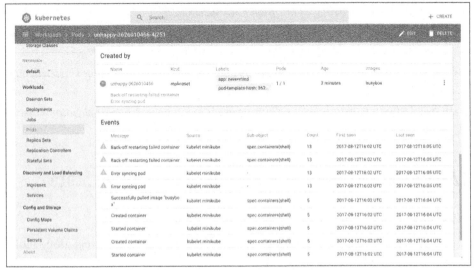

Figure 12-2. Screenshot of pod in error state

Discussion

An issue, be it a pod failing or a node behaving strangely, can have many different causes. Here are some things you'll want to check before suspecting software bugs:

- Is the manifest correct? Check with the Kubernetes JSON schema (*https://github.com/garethr/kubernetes-json-schema*).
- Does the container run standalone, locally (that is, outside of Kubernetes)?
- Can Kubernetes reach the container registry and actually pull the container image?
- Can the nodes talk to each other?
- Can the nodes reach the master?
- Is DNS available in the cluster?

- Are there sufficient resources available on the nodes?
- Did you restrict the container's resource usage (*https://hackernoon.com/container-resource-consumption-too-important-to-ignore-7484609a3bb7*)?

See Also

- Kubernetes Troubleshoot Applications documentation (*https://kubernetes.io/docs/tasks/debug-application-cluster/debug-application/*)
- Application Introspection and Debugging (*https://kubernetes.io/docs/tasks/debug-application-cluster/debug-application-introspection/*)
- Debug Pods and Replication Controllers (*https://kubernetes.io/docs/tasks/debug-application-cluster/debug-pod-replication-controller/*)
- Debug Services (*https://kubernetes.io/docs/tasks/debug-application-cluster/debug-service/*)
- Troubleshoot Clusters (*https://kubernetes.io/docs/tasks/debug-application-cluster/debug-cluster/*)

12.6 Getting a Detailed Snapshot of the Cluster State

Problem

You want to get a detailed snapshot of the overall cluster state for orientation, auditing, or troubleshooting purposes.

Solution

Use the kubectl cluster-info dump command. For example, to create a dump of the cluster state in a subdirectory *cluster-state-2017-08-13*, do this:

```
$ kubectl cluster-info dump --all-namespaces \
  --output-directory=$PWD/cluster-state-2017-08-13

$ tree ./cluster-state-2017-08-13
.
├── default
│   ├── cockroachdb-0
│   │   └── logs.txt
│   ├── cockroachdb-1
│   │   └── logs.txt
│   ├── cockroachdb-2
│   │   └── logs.txt
│   ├── daemonsets.json
│   ├── deployments.json
```

```
│     ├── events.json
│     ├── jump-1247516000-sz87w
│     │     └── logs.txt
│     ├── nginx-4217019353-462mb
│     │     └── logs.txt
│     ├── nginx-4217019353-z3g8d
│     │     └── logs.txt
│     ├── pods.json
│     ├── prom-2436944326-pr60g
│     │     └── logs.txt
│     ├── replicasets.json
│     ├── replication-controllers.json
│     └── services.json
├── kube-public
│     ├── daemonsets.json
│     ├── deployments.json
│     ├── events.json
│     ├── pods.json
│     ├── replicasets.json
│     ├── replication-controllers.json
│     └── services.json
├── kube-system
│     ├── daemonsets.json
│     ├── default-http-backend-wdfwc
│     │     └── logs.txt
│     ├── deployments.json
│     ├── events.json
│     ├── kube-addon-manager-minikube
│     │     └── logs.txt
│     ├── kube-dns-910330662-dvr9f
│     │     └── logs.txt
│     ├── kubernetes-dashboard-5pqmk
│     │     └── logs.txt
│     ├── nginx-ingress-controller-d2f2z
│     │     └── logs.txt
│     ├── pods.json
│     ├── replicasets.json
│     ├── replication-controllers.json
│     └── services.json
└── nodes.json
```

12.7 Adding Kubernetes Worker Nodes

Problem

You need to add a worker node to your Kubernetes cluster.

Solution

Provision a new machine in whatever way your environment requires (for example, in a bare-metal environment you might need to physically install a new server in a rack, in a public cloud setting you need to create a new VM, etc.), and then install the three components that make up a Kubernetes worker node:

kubelet
> This is the node manager and supervisor for all pods, no matter if they're controlled by the API server or running locally, such as static pods. Note that the kubelet is the final arbiter of what pods can or cannot run on a given node, and takes care of:
>
> - Reporting node and pod statuses to the API server.
> - Periodically executing liveness probes.
> - Mounting the pod volumes and downloading secrets.
> - Controlling the container runtime (see the following).

Container runtime
> This is responsible for downloading container images and running the containers. Initially, this was hardwired to the Docker engine, but nowadays it is a pluggable system based on the Container Runtime Interface (CRI) (*https://github.com/kubernetes/community/blob/master/contributors/devel/container-runtime-interface.md*), so you can, for example, use CRI-O (*http://cri-o.io/*) rather than Docker.

kube-proxy
> This process dynamically configures iptables rules on the node to enable the Kubernetes service abstraction (redirecting the VIP to the endpoints, one or more pods representing the service).

The actual installation of the components depends heavily on your environment and the installation method used (cloud, kubeadm, etc.). For a list of available options, see the kubelet reference (*https://kubernetes.io/docs/admin/kubelet/*) and kube-proxy reference (*https://kubernetes.io/docs/admin/kube-proxy/*).

Discussion

Worker nodes, unlike other Kubernetes resources such as a deployments or services, are not directly created by the Kubernetes control plane but only managed by it. That means when Kubernetes creates a node, it actually only creates an object that *represents* the worker node. It validates the node by health checks based on the node's metadata.name field, and if the node is valid—that is, all necessary components are running—it is considered part of the cluster; otherwise, it will be ignored for any cluster activity until it becomes valid.

See Also

- "The Kubernetes Node" (*https://github.com/kubernetes/community/blob/master/ contributors/design-proposals/architecture/architecture.md#the-kubernetes-node*) in the Kubernetes Architecture design document
- Master-Node communication (*https://kubernetes.io/docs/concepts/architecture/ master-node-communication/*)
- Static Pods (*https://kubernetes.io/docs/tasks/administer-cluster/static-pod/*)

12.8 Draining Kubernetes Nodes for Maintenance

Problem

You need to carry out maintenance on a node—for example, to apply a security patch or upgrade the operating system.

Solution

Use the `kubectl drain` command. For example, to do maintenance on node `123-worker`:

```
$ kubectl drain 123-worker
```

When you are ready to put the node back into service, use `kubectl uncordon 123-worker`, which will make the node schedulable again.

Discussion

What the `kubectl drain` command does is to first mark the specified node unschedulable to prevent new pods from arriving (essentially a `kubectl cordon`). Then it evicts the pods if the API server supports eviction (*http://kubernetes.io/docs/admin/ disruptions/*). Otherwise, it will use normal `kubectl delete` to delete the pods. The Kubernetes docs have a concise sequence diagram of the steps, reproduced in Figure 12-3.

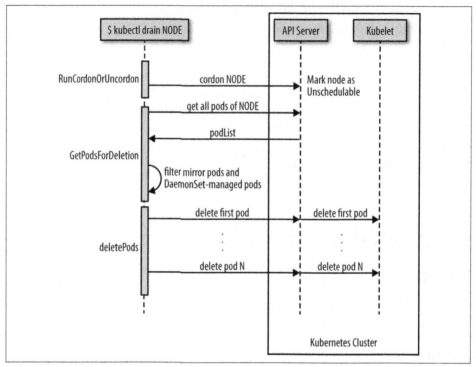

Figure 12-3. Node drain sequence diagram

The `kubectl drain` command evicts or deletes all pods except mirror pods (which cannot be deleted through the API server). For pods supervised by a `DaemonSet`, drain will not proceed without using `--ignore-daemonsets`, and regardless it will not delete any `DaemonSet`-managed pods—those pods would be immediately replaced by the `DaemonSet` controller, which ignores unschedulable markings.

 `drain` waits for graceful termination, so you should not operate on this node until the `kubectl drain` command has completed. Note that `kubectl drain $NODE --force` will also evict pods not managed by an RC, RS, job, `DaemonSet`, or `StatefulSet`.

See Also

- Safely Drain a Node while Respecting Application SLOs (*https://kubernetes.io/docs/tasks/administer-cluster/safely-drain-node/*)

- The `kubectl` reference docs (*https://kubernetes.io/docs/reference/generated/kubectl/kubectl-commands#drain*)

12.9 Managing etcd

Problem

You need to access etcd to back it up or verify the cluster state directly.

Solution

Get access to etcd and query it, either using curl or etcdctl (*https://github.com/coreos/etcd/tree/master/etcdctl*). For example, in the context of Minikube (with jq installed):

```
$ minikube ssh

$ curl 127.0.0.1:2379/v2/keys/registry | jq .
{
  "action": "get",
  "node": {
    "key": "/registry",
    "dir": true,
    "nodes": [
      {
        "key": "/registry/persistentvolumeclaims",
        "dir": true,
        "modifiedIndex": 241330,
        "createdIndex": 241330
      },
      {
        "key": "/registry/apiextensions.k8s.io",
        "dir": true,
        "modifiedIndex": 641,
        "createdIndex": 641
      },
  ...
```

This technique can be used in environments where etcd is used with the v2 API (*https://coreos.com/etcd/docs/latest/v2/README.html*).

Discussion

In Kubernetes, etcd is a component of the control plane. The API server (see Recipe 6.1) is stateless and the only Kubernetes component that directly communicates with etcd, the distributed storage component that manages the cluster state. Essentially, etcd is a key/value store; in etcd2 the keys formed a hierarchy, but with the introduction of etcd3 (*https://coreos.com/blog/etcd3-a-new-etcd.html*) this was replaced with a flat model (while maintaining backwards compatibility concerning hierarchical keys).

Up until Kubernetes 1.5.2 we used `etcd2`, and from then on we switched to `etcd3`. In Kubernetes 1.5.x, `etcd3` is still used in v2 API mode and going forward this is changing to the etcd v3 API with v2 being deprecated soon. Though from a developer's point of view this doesn't have any implications, because the API server takes care of abstracting the interactions away, as an admin you want to pay attention to which etcd version is used in which API mode.

In general, it's the responsibility of the cluster admin to manage `etcd`—that is, to upgrade it and make sure the data is backed up. In certain environments where the control plane is managed for you, such as in Google Kubernetes Engine, you cannot access `etcd` directly. This is by design, and there's no workaround for it.

See Also

- etcd v2 Cluster Administration guide (*https://coreos.com/etcd/docs/latest/v2/admin_guide.html*)

- etcd v3 Disaster Recovery guide (*https://coreos.com/etcd/docs/latest/op-guide/recovery.html*)

- Operating etcd clusters for Kubernetes (*https://kubernetes.io/docs/tasks/administer-cluster/configure-upgrade-etcd/*)

- "Accessing Localkube Resources from Inside a Pod: Example etcd" (*https://github.com/kubernetes/minikube/blob/master/docs/accessing_etcd.md*) in the Minikube docs

- Stefan Schimanski and Michael Hausenblas's blog post "Kubernetes Deep Dive: API Server – Part 2" (*https://blog.openshift.com/kubernetes-deep-dive-api-server-part-2/*)

- Michael Hausenblas's blog post "Notes on Moving from etcd2 to etcd3" (*https://hackernoon.com/notes-on-moving-from-etcd2-to-etcd3-dedb26057b90*)

## CHAPTER 13

Developing Kubernetes

Now that you've seen how to install, interact with, and use Kubernetes to deploy and manage applications, we focus in this chapter on adapting Kubernetes to your needs as well as fixing bugs in Kubernetes. For this, you will need Go (*http://golang.org*) installed and access to the Kubernetes source code hosted on GitHub (*https://github.com/kubernetes/kubernetes*). We show how to compile Kubernetes (as a whole) and also show how to compile specific components like the client kubectl. We also demonstrate how to use Python to talk to the Kubernetes API server and show how to extend Kubernetes with a custom resource definition.

13.1 Compiling from Source

Problem

You want to package your own Kubernetes binaries from source instead of downloading the official release binaries (see Recipe 2.4) or third-party artifacts.

Solution

Clone the Kubernetes Git repository and build from source.

If you are on a Docker host, you can use the quick-release target of the root *Makefile* as shown here:

```
$ git clone https://github.com/kubernetes/kubernetes
$ cd kubernetes
$ make quick-release
```

This Docker-based build requires at least 4 GB of RAM to complete. Ensure that your Docker daemon has access to that much memory. On macOS, access the Docker for Mac preferences and increase the allocated RAM.

The binaries will be located in the _output/release-stage directory and a complete bundle will be in the _output/release-tars directory.

Or, if you have a Golang (*https://golang.org/doc/install*) environment properly set up, use the release target of the root *Makefile*:

```
$ git clone https://github.com/kubernetes/Kubernetes
$ cd kubernetes
$ make
```

The binaries will be located in the _output/bin directory.

See Also

- Detailed Kubernetes developer guides (*https://github.com/kubernetes/community/tree/master/contributors/devel*)

13.2 Compiling a Specific Component

Problem

You want to build a specific component of Kubernetes from source, not all the components—for example, you only want to build the client kubectl.

Solution

Instead of using make quick-release or simply make, as shown in Recipe 13.1, do make kubectl.

There are targets in the root *Makefile* to build individual components. For example to compile kubectl, kubeadm, and hyperkube, do this:

```
$ make kubectl
$ make kubeadm
$ make hyperkube
```

The binaries will be located in the _output/bin directory.

13.3 Using a Python Client to Interact with the Kubernetes API

Problem

You want to use Python to write scripts that use the Kubernetes API.

Solution

Install the Python kubernetes module. This module is currently being developed in the Kubernetes incubator (*https://github.com/kubernetes-incubator/client-python*). You can install the module from source or from the Python Package Index (PyPi) site (*https://pypi.python.org/pypi*):

```
$ pip install kubernetes
```

With a Kubernetes cluster reachable using your default kubectl context, you are now ready to use this Python module to talk to the Kubernetes API. For example, the following Python script lists all the pods and prints their names:

```
from kubernetes import client, config

config.load_kube_config()

v1 = client.CoreV1Api()
res = v1.list_pod_for_all_namespaces(watch=False)
for pod in res.items:
    print(pod.metadata.name)
```

The config.load_kube_config() call in this script will load your Kubernetes credentials and endpoint from your kubectl config file. By default, it will load the cluster endpoint and credentials for your current context.

Discussion

The Python client is built using the OpenAPI specification of the Kubernetes API. It is up to date and autogenerated. All APIs are available through this client.

Each API group corresponds to a specific class, so to call a method on an API object that is part of the /api/v1 API group, you need to instantiate the CoreV1Api class. To use deployments, you will need to instantiate the extensionsV1beta1Api class. All methods and corresponding API group instances can be found in the autogenerated *README* (*https://github.com/kubernetes-incubator/client-python/tree/master/kubernetes*).

See Also

- Examples in the project's repository (*https://github.com/kubernetes-incubator/client-python/tree/master/examples*)

13.4 Extending the API Using Custom Resource Definitions (CRDs)

Problem

You have a custom workload and none of the existing resources, such as Deployment, a Job, or a StatefulSet, is a good fit. So, you want to extend the Kubernetes API with a new resource that represents your workload while continuing to use kubectl in the usual way.

Solution

Use a CustomResourceDefinition (CRD) (*https://kubernetes.io/docs/concepts/api-extension/custom-resources/*) as described [here].

Let's say you want to define a custom resource of kind Function. This represents a short-running Job-like kind of resource, akin to what AWS Lambda offers, that is a Function-as-a-Service (FaaS, or sometimes misleadingly called "serverless").

For a production-ready FaaS solution running on Kubernetes, see Recipe 14.7.

First, define the CRD in a manifest file called *functions-crd.yaml*:

```
apiVersion: apiextensions.k8s.io/v1beta1
kind:       CustomResourceDefinition
metadata:
  name:     function.example.com
spec:
  group:    example.com
  version:  v1
  names:
    kind:   Function
    plural: functions
    scope:  Namespaced
```

Then let the API server know about your new CRD (it can take several minutes to register):

```
$ kubectl create -f functions-crd.yaml
customresourcedefinition "functions.example.com" created
```

Now that you have the custom resource Function defined and the API server knows about it, you can instantiate it using a manifest called *myfaas.yaml* with the following content:

```
apiVersion: example.com/v1
kind:       Function
metadata:
  name:     myfaas
spec:
  code:     "http://src.example.com/myfaas.js"
  ram:      100Mi
```

And create the myfaas resource of kind Function as per usual:

```
$ kubectl create -f myfaas.yaml
function "myfaas" created
```

```
$ kubectl get crd functions.example.com -o yaml
apiVersion: apiextensions.k8s.io/v1beta1
kind: CustomResourceDefinition
metadata:
  creationTimestamp: 2017-08-13T10:11:50Z
  name: functions.example.com
  resourceVersion: "458065"
  selfLink: /apis/apiextensions.k8s.io/v1beta1/customresourcedefinitions
            /functions.example.com
  uid: 278016fe-81a2-11e7-b58a-080027390640
spec:
  group: example.com
  names:
    kind: Function
    listKind: FunctionList
    plural: functions
    singular: function
  scope: Namespaced
  version: v1
status:
  acceptedNames:
    kind: Function
    listKind: FunctionList
    plural: functions
    singular: function
  conditions:
  - lastTransitionTime: null
    message: no conflicts found
    reason: NoConflicts
    status: "True"
```

```
      type: NamesAccepted
    - lastTransitionTime: 2017-08-13T10:11:50Z
      message: the initial names have been accepted
      reason: InitialNamesAccepted
      status: "True"
      type: Established

$ kubectl describe functions.example.com/myfaas
Name:          myfaas
Namespace:     default
Labels:        <none>
Annotations:   <none>
API Version:   example.com/v1
Kind:          Function
Metadata:
  Cluster Name:
  Creation Timestamp:                2017-08-13T10:12:07Z
  Deletion Grace Period Seconds:     <nil>
  Deletion Timestamp:                <nil>
  Resource Version:                  458086
  Self Link:                         /apis/example.com/v1/namespaces/default
                                     /functions/myfaas
  UID:                               316f3e99-81a2-11e7-b58a-080027390640
Spec:
  Code: http://src.example.com/myfaas.js
  Ram:  100Mi
Events: <none>
```

To discover CRDs, simply access the API server. For example, using kubectl proxy, you can access the API server locally and query the key space (example.com/v1 in our case):

```
$ curl 127.0.0.1:8001/apis/example.com/v1/ | jq .
{
  "kind": "APIResourceList",
  "apiVersion": "v1",
  "groupVersion": "example.com/v1",
  "resources": [
    {
      "name": "functions",
      "singularName": "function",
      "namespaced": true,
      "kind": "Function",
      "verbs": [
        "delete",
        "deletecollection",
        "get",
        "list",
        "patch",
        "create",
        "update",
        "watch"
```

```
        ]
      }
    ]
  }
```

Here you can see the resource along with the allowed verbs.

When you want to get rid of your custom resource instance `myfaas`, simply delete it:

```
$ kubectl delete functions.example.com/myfaas
function "myfaas" deleted
```

Discussion

As you've seen, it is straightforward to create a CRD. From an end user's point of view, CRDs present a consistent API and are more or less indistinguishable from native resources such as pods or jobs. All the usual commands, such as `kubectl get` and `kubectl delete`, work as expected.

Creating a CRD is, however, really less than half of the work necessary to fully extend the Kubernetes API. On their own, CRDs only let you store and retrieve custom data via the API server in etcd. You need to also write a custom controller (*https://engineer ing.bitnami.com/articles/a-deep-dive-into-kubernetes-controllers.html*) that interprets the custom data expressing the user's intent and establishes a control loop comparing the current state with the declared state, and tries to reconcile both.

 Up until v1.7, what are now known as CRDs were called *third-party resources* (TPRs). If you happen to have a TPR, strongly consider migrating (*https://kubernetes.io/docs/tasks/access-kubernetes-api/ migrate-third-party-resource/*) it now.

The main limitations of CRDs (and hence the reasons you might want to use a user API server in certain cases) are:

- Only a single version per CRD is supported, though it is possible to have multiple versions per API group (that means you can't convert between different representations of your CRD).

- CRDS don't support assigning default values to fields in v1.7 or earlier.

- Validation of the fields defined in a CRD specification is possible only from v1.8.

- It's not possible to define subresources, such as `status` resources.

See Also

- Extend the Kubernetes API with CustomResourceDefinitions (*https://kubernetes.io/docs/tasks/access-kubernetes-api/extend-api-custom-resource-definitions/*)
- Stefan Schimanski and Michael Hausenblas's blog post "Kubernetes Deep Dive: API Server – Part 3a" (*https://blog.openshift.com/kubernetes-deep-dive-api-server-part-3a/*)
- Aaron Levy, "Writing a Custom Controller: Extending the Functionality of Your Cluster" (*https://www.youtube.com/watch?v=_BuqPMlXfpE*), KubeCon 2017
- Tu Nguyen's article "A Deep Dive into Kubernetes Controllers" (*https://engineering.bitnami.com/articles/a-deep-dive-into-kubernetes-controllers.html*)
- Yaron Haviv's article "Extend Kubernetes 1.7 with Custom Resources" (*https://thenewstack.io/extend-kubernetes-1-7-custom-resources/*)

## CHAPTER 14

The Ecosystem

In this chapter, we take a look at the wider Kubernetes ecosystem; that is, software in the Kubernetes incubator (*https://github.com/kubernetes-incubator*) and related projects such as Helm (*https://helm.sh*) and kompose (*http://kompose.io/*).

14.1 Installing Helm, the Kubernetes Package Manager

Problem

You do not want to write all the Kubernetes manifests by hand. Instead, you would like to be able to search for a package in a repository and download and install it with a command-line interface.

Solution

Use Helm (*https://github.com/kubernetes/helm*). Helm is the Kubernetes package manager; it defines a Kubernetes package as a set of manifests and some metadata. The manifests are actually templates. The values in the templates are filled when the package is instantiated by Helm. A Helm package is called a chart.

Helm has a client-side CLI called helm and a server called tiller. You interact with charts using helm, and tiller runs within your Kubernetes cluster as a regular Kubernetes deployment.

You can build Helm from source or download it from the GitHub release page (*https://github.com/kubernetes/helm/releases*), extract the archive, and move the helm binary into your $PATH. For example, on macOS, for the v2.7.2 release of Helm, do this:

```
$ wget https://storage.googleapis.com/kubernetes-helm/ \
  helm-v2.7.2-darwin-amd64.tar.gz

$ tar -xvf helm-v2.7.2-darwin-amd64.tar.gz

$ sudo mv darwin-amd64/64 /usr/local/bin

$ helm version
```

Now that the `helm` command is in your $PATH, you can use it to start the server-side component, `tiller`, on your Kubernetes cluster. Here we use Minikube as an example:

```
$ kubectl get nodes
NAME       STATUS   AGE      VERSION
minikube   Ready    4m       v1.7.8

$ helm init
$HELM_HOME has been configured at /Users/sebgoa/.helm.

Tiller (the helm server side component) has been installed into your Kubernetes
Cluster. Happy Helming!

$ kubectl get pods --all-namespaces | grep tiller
kube-system   tiller-deploy-1491950541-4kqxx   0/1 ContainerCreating 0 1s
```

You're all set now and can install one of the over 100 packages available (*https://hub.kubeapps.com/*).

14.2 Using Helm to Install Applications

Problem

You've installed the `helm` command (see Recipe 14.1), and now you would like to search for charts and deploy them.

Solution

By default, Helm comes with some chart repositories configured. These repositories are maintained by the community; you can read more about them on GitHub (*https://github.com/kubernetes/charts*). There are over 100 charts available.

For example, let's assume you would like to deploy Redis. You can search for `redis` in the Helm repositories and then install it. Helm will take the chart and create an instance of it called a *release*.

First, verify that `tiller` is running and that you have the default repositories configured:

```
$ kubectl get pods --all-namespaces | grep tiller
kube-system    tiller-deploy-1491950541-4kqxx   1/1   Running   0   3m

$ helm repo list
NAME    URL
stable  http://storage.googleapis.com/kubernetes-charts
```

You can now search for a Redis package:

```
$ helm search redis
NAME                      VERSION   DESCRIPTION
stable/redis              0.5.1     Open source, advanced key-value store. It ...
testing/redis-cluster     0.0.5     Highly available Redis cluster with multiple...
testing/redis-standalone  0.0.1     Standalone Redis Master
stable/sensu              0.1.2     Sensu monitoring framework backed by the ...
testing/example-todo      0.0.6     Example Todo application backed by Redis
```

And use `helm install` to create a release like so:

```
$ helm install stable/redis
```

Helm will create all the Kubernetes objects defined in the chart; for example, a secret (see Recipe 8.2), a PVC (see Recipe 8.5), a service (see Recipe 5.1), and/or a deployment. Together, these objects make up a Helm release that you can manage as a single unit.

The end result is that you will have a `redis` pod running:

```
$ helm ls
NAME           REVISION   UPDATED                      STATUS     CHART          ...
broken-badger  1          Fri May 12 11:50:43 2017     DEPLOYED   redis-0.5.1    ...

$ kubectl get pods
NAME                                    READY   STATUS    RESTARTS   AGE
broken-badger-redis-4040604371-tcn14    1/1     Running   0          3m
```

To learn more about Helm charts and how to create your own charts, see Recipe 14.3.

14.3 Creating Your Own Chart to Package Your Application with Helm

Problem

You have written an application with multiple Kubernetes manifests and would like to package it as a Helm chart.

Solution

Use the `helm create` and `helm package` commands.

With `helm create`, you can generate the skeleton of your chart. Issue the command in your terminal, specifying the name of your chart. For example, to create an `oreilly` chart:

```
$ helm create oreilly
Creating oreilly

$ tree oreilly/
oreilly/
├── Chart.yaml
├── charts
├── templates
│   ├── NOTES.txt
│   ├── _helpers.tpl
│   ├── deployment.yaml
│   ├── ingress.yaml
│   └── service.yaml
└── values.yaml

2 directories, 7 files
```

If you have all your manifests already written, you can copy them into the */templates* directory and delete what the scaffolding created. If you want to templatize your manifests, then write the values that need to be substituted in the manifests in the *values.yaml* file. Edit the metadata file *Chart.yaml*, and if you have any dependent charts put them in the */charts* directory.

You can test your chart locally by running:

```
$ helm install ./oreilly
```

Finally, you can package it with `helm package oreilly/`. This will generate a tarball of your chart, copy it to a local chart repository, and generate a new *index.yaml* file for your local repository. Look into the *~/.helm* directory and you should see something similar to the following:

```
$ ls -l ~/.helm/repository/local/
total 16
-rw-r--r--  1 sebgoa  staff   379 Dec 16 21:25 index.yaml
-rw-r--r--  1 sebgoa  staff  1321 Dec 16 21:25 oreilly-0.1.0.tgz
```

A `helm search oreilly` should now return your local chart:

```
$ helm search oreilly
NAME            VERSION   DESCRIPTION
local/oreilly   0.1.0     A Helm chart for Kubernetes
```

See Also

- "How to Create Your First Helm Chart" (*https://docs.bitnami.com/kubernetes/ how-to/create-your-first-helm-chart/*) in the Bitnami docs for Kubernetes

- "The Chart Best Practices Guide" (*https://docs.helm.sh/chart_best_practices/*) in the Helm docs

14.4 Converting Your Docker Compose Files to Kubernetes Manifests

Problem

You've started using containers with Docker and written some Docker compose files to define your multicontainer application. Now you would like to start using Kubernetes, and wonder if and how you can reuse your Docker compose files.

Solution

Use kompose, a CLI tool that converts your Docker compose files into Kubernetes manifests.

To start, download kompose from the GitHub release page (*https://github.com/kubernetes-incubator/kompose/releases*) and move it to your $PATH, for convenience.

For example, on macOS, do the following:

```
$ wget https://github.com/kubernetes-incubator/kompose/releases/download/ \
    v1.6.0/kompose-darwin-amd64

$ sudo mv kompose-darwin-amd64 /usr/local/bin/kompose

$ sudo chmod +x /usr/local/bin/kompose

$ kompose version
1.6.0 (ae4ef9e)
```

Given the following Docker compose file that starts a redis container:

```
version: '2'

services:
  redis:
    image: redis
    ports:
    - "6379:6379"
```

You can automatically convert this into Kubernetes manifests with the following command:

```
$ kompose convert --stdout
```

The manifests will be printed to `stdout` and you will see a Kubernetes service and a deployment as a result. To create these objects automatically, you can use the Docker compose-compliant command up like so:

```
$ kompose up
```

 Some Docker compose directives are not converted to Kubernetes. In this case, `kompose` prints out a warning informing you that the conversion did not happen.

While in general it doesn't cause problems, it is possible that the conversion may not result in a working manifest in Kubernetes. This is expected as this type of transformation cannot be perfect. However, it gets you close to a working Kubernetes manifest. Most notably, handling volumes and network isolation will typically require manual, custom work from your side.

Discussion

The main `kompose` commands are `convert`, `up`, and `down`. You can view detailed help for each command in the CLI using the `--help` option.

By default, `kompose` converts your Docker services into a Kubernetes deployment and associated service. You can also specify the use of a `DaemonSet` (see Recipe 7.3), or you can use OpenShift-specific objects such as a `DeploymentConfiguration` (*https:// docs.openshift.org/latest/architecture/core_concepts/deployments.html#deployments- and-deployment-configurations*).

14.5 Creating a Kubernetes Cluster with kubicorn

Problem

You want to create a Kubernetes cluster on AWS.

Solution

Use `kubicorn` (*https://github.com/kris-nova/kubicorn*) to create and manage Kubernetes clusters on AWS. Since `kubicorn` currently doesn't provide for binary releases, you need to have Go installed (*https://golang.org/dl/*) for the following to work.

First, install `kubicorn` and make sure that Go (version 1.8 or later) is available. Here, we're using a CentOS environment.

```
$ go version
go version go1.8 linux/amd64

$ yum group install "Development Tools" \
```

```
yum install ncurses-devel
```

```
$ go get github.com/kris-nova/kubicorn
...
Create, Manage, Image, and Scale Kubernetes infrastructure in the cloud.

Usage:
  kubicorn [flags]
  kubicorn [command]

Available Commands:
  adopt        Adopt a Kubernetes cluster into a Kubicorn state store
  apply        Apply a cluster resource to a cloud
  completion   Generate completion code for bash and zsh shells.
  create       Create a Kubicorn API model from a profile
  delete       Delete a Kubernetes cluster
  getconfig    Manage Kubernetes configuration
  help         Help about any command
  image        Take an image of a Kubernetes cluster
  list         List available states
  version      Verify Kubicorn version

Flags:
  -C, --color       Toggle colorized logs (default true)
  -f, --fab         Toggle colorized logs
  -h, --help        help for kubicorn
  -v, --verbose int Log level (default 3)

Use "kubicorn [command] --help" for more information about a command.
```

Once you have the kubicorn command installed, you can create the cluster resources by selecting a *profile* and verifying whether the resources are properly defined:

```
$ kubicorn create --name k8scb --profile aws
2017-08-14T05:18:24Z [✓]  Selected [fs] state store
2017-08-14T05:18:24Z [✿]  The state [./_state/k8scb/cluster.yaml] has been...

$ cat _state/k8scb/cluster.yaml
SSH:
  Identifier: ""
  metadata:
    creationTimestamp: null
  publicKeyPath: ~/.ssh/id_rsa.pub
  user: ubuntu
cloud: amazon
kubernetesAPI:
  metadata:
    creationTimestamp: null
  port: "443"
location: us-west-2
...
```

The default resource profile we're using assumes you have a key pair in ~/.ssh named id_rsa (private key) and id_rsa.pub (public key). If this is not the case, you might want to change this. Also, note that the default region used is Oregon, us-west-2.

To continue, you need to have an AWS Identity and Access Management (IAM) user with the following permissions available: AmazonEC2FullAccess, AutoScalingFullAccess, and AmazonVPCFullAccess. If you don't have such an IAM user, now is a good time to create one.[1]

One last thing you need to do for kubicorn to work is set the credentials of the IAM user you're using (see previous step) as environment variables, as follows:

```
$ export AWS_ACCESS_KEY_ID=***************************
$ export AWS_SECRET_ACCESS_KEY=****************************************
```

Now you're in a position to create the cluster, based on the resource definitions above as well as the AWS access you provided:

```
$ kubicorn apply --name k8scb
2017-08-14T05:45:04Z [✓]  Selected [fs] state store
2017-08-14T05:45:04Z [✓]  Loaded cluster: k8scb
2017-08-14T05:45:04Z [✓]  Init Cluster
2017-08-14T05:45:04Z [✓]  Query existing resources
2017-08-14T05:45:04Z [✓]  Resolving expected resources
2017-08-14T05:45:04Z [✓]  Reconciling
2017-08-14T05:45:07Z [✓]  Created KeyPair [k8scb]
2017-08-14T05:45:08Z [✓]  Created VPC [vpc-7116a317]
2017-08-14T05:45:09Z [✓]  Created Internet Gateway [igw-e88c148f]
2017-08-14T05:45:09Z [✓]  Attaching Internet Gateway [igw-e88c148f] to VPC ...
2017-08-14T05:45:10Z [✓]  Created Security Group [sg-11dba36b]
2017-08-14T05:45:11Z [✓]  Created Subnet [subnet-50c0d919]
2017-08-14T05:45:11Z [✓]  Created Route Table [rtb-8fd9dae9]
2017-08-14T05:45:11Z [✓]  Mapping route table [rtb-8fd9dae9] to internet gate...
2017-08-14T05:45:12Z [✓]  Associated route table [rtb-8fd9dae9] to subnet ...
2017-08-14T05:45:15Z [✓]  Created Launch Configuration [k8scb.master]
2017-08-14T05:45:16Z [✓]  Created Asg [k8scb.master]
2017-08-14T05:45:16Z [✓]  Created Security Group [sg-e8dca492]
2017-08-14T05:45:17Z [✓]  Created Subnet [subnet-cccfd685]
2017-08-14T05:45:17Z [✓]  Created Route Table [rtb-76dcdf10]
2017-08-14T05:45:18Z [✓]  Mapping route table [rtb-76dcdf10] to internet gate...
2017-08-14T05:45:19Z [✓]  Associated route table [rtb-76dcdf10] to subnet ...
2017-08-14T05:45:54Z [✓]  Found public IP for master: [34.213.102.27]
2017-08-14T05:45:58Z [✓]  Created Launch Configuration [k8scb.node]
2017-08-14T05:45:58Z [✓]  Created Asg [k8scb.node]
2017-08-14T05:45:59Z [✓]  Updating state store for cluster [k8scb]
```

---

1 AWS Identity and Access Management User Guide, "Creating an IAM User in Your AWS Account" (*http://docs.aws.amazon.com/IAM/latest/UserGuide/id_users_create.html*).

```
2017-08-14T05:47:13Z [✿]  Wrote kubeconfig to [/root/.kube/config]
2017-08-14T05:47:14Z [✿]  The [k8scb] cluster has applied successfully!
2017-08-14T05:47:14Z [✿]  You can now `kubectl get nodes`
2017-08-14T05:47:14Z [✿]  You can SSH into your cluster ssh -i ~/.ssh/id_rsa ...
```

Although you don't see the beautiful coloring here, the last four lines of output are green and tell you that everything has been successfully set up. You can also verify this by visiting the Amazon EC2 console in a browser, as shown in Figure 14-1.

Figure 14-1. Screenshot of Amazon EC2 console, showing two nodes created by kubicorn

Now, do as instructed in the last output line of the `kubicorn apply` command and ssh into the cluster:

```
$ ssh -i ~/.ssh/id_rsa ubuntu@34.213.102.27
The authenticity of host '34.213.102.27 (34.213.102.27)' can't be established.
ECDSA key fingerprint is ed:89:6b:86:d9:f0:2e:3e:50:2a:d4:09:62:f6:70:bc.
Are you sure you want to continue connecting (yes/no)? yes
Warning: Permanently added '34.213.102.27' (ECDSA) to the list of known hosts.
Welcome to Ubuntu 16.04.2 LTS (GNU/Linux 4.4.0-1020-aws x86_64)

 * Documentation:  https://help.ubuntu.com
 * Management:     https://landscape.canonical.com
 * Support:        https://ubuntu.com/advantage

  Get cloud support with Ubuntu Advantage Cloud Guest:
    http://www.ubuntu.com/business/services/cloud

75 packages can be updated.
32 updates are security updates.
```

```
To run a command as administrator (user "root"), use "sudo <command>".
See "man sudo_root" for details.

ubuntu@ip-10-0-0-52:~$ kubectl get all -n kube-system
NAME                                              READY   STATUS
po/calico-etcd-qr3f1                              1/1     Running
po/calico-node-9t472                              2/2     Running
po/calico-node-qlpp6                              2/2     Running
po/calico-policy-controller-1727037546-f152z      1/1     Running
po/etcd-ip-10-0-0-52                              1/1     Running
po/kube-apiserver-ip-10-0-0-52                    1/1     Running
po/kube-controller-manager-ip-10-0-0-52           1/1     Running
po/kube-dns-2425271678-zcfdd                      0/3     ContainerCreating
po/kube-proxy-3s2c0                               1/1     Running
po/kube-proxy-t10ck                               1/1     Running
po/kube-scheduler-ip-10-0-0-52                    1/1     Running

NAME             CLUSTER-IP      EXTERNAL-IP   PORT(S)         AGE
svc/calico-etcd  10.96.232.136   <none>        6666/TCP        4m
svc/kube-dns     10.96.0.10      <none>        53/UDP,53/TCP   4m

NAME                             DESIRED   CURRENT   UP-TO-DATE   AVAILABLE   AGE
deploy/calico-policy-controller  1         1         1            1           4m
deploy/kube-dns                  1         1         1            0           4m

NAME                                     DESIRED   CURRENT   READY   AGE
rs/calico-policy-controller-1727037546   1         1         1       4m
rs/kube-dns-2425271678                   1         1         0       4m
```

When you're done, tear down the Kubernetes cluster like so (note that this may take a
couple of minutes):

```
$ kubicorn delete --name k8scb
2017-08-14T05:53:38Z [✓]  Selected [fs] state store
Destroying resources for cluster [k8scb]:
2017-08-14T05:53:41Z [✓]  Deleted ASG [k8scb.node]
...
2017-08-14T05:55:42Z [✓]  Deleted VPC [vpc-7116a317]
```

Discussion

While kubicorn is a rather young project, it is fully functional, and you can also create clusters on Azure (*http://kubicorn.io/documentation/azure-walkthrough.html*) and
Digital Ocean (*http://kubicorn.io/documentation/do-walkthrough.html*) with it.

It does require you to have Go installed as it doesn't ship binaries (yet), but it's very
flexible in terms of configuration and also rather intuitive to handle, especially if you
have an admin background.

See Also

- Setting up Kubernetes in AWS (*http://kubicorn.io/documentation/aws-walkthrough.html*) in the kubicorn docs
- Lachlan Evenson's video walk-through "Building a Kubernetes Cluster on Digital Ocean Using Kubicorn" (*https://www.youtube.com/watch?v=XpxgSZ3dspE*)

14.6 Storing Encrypted Secrets in Version Control

Problem

You want to store all your Kubernetes manifests in version control and safely share them (even publicly), including secrets.

Solution

Use sealed-secrets (*https://github.com/bitnami/sealed-secrets*). Sealed-secrets is a Kubernetes controller that decrypts one-way encrypted secrets and creates in-cluster Secret objects (see Recipe 8.2).

Your sensitive information is encrypted into a SealedSecret object, which is a custom CRD resource (see Recipe 13.4). The SealedSecret is safe to store under version control and share even publicly. Once a SealedSecret is created on the Kubernetes API server, the controller decrypts it and creates the corresponding Secret object (which is only base64-encoded).

To get started, download the latest release of the kubeseal binary. This will allow you to encrypt your secrets:

```
$ GOOS=$(go env GOOS)

$ GOARCH=$(go env GOARCH)

$ wget https://github.com/bitnami/sealed-secrets/releases/download/v0.5.1/
    kubeseal-$GOOS-$GOARCH

$ sudo install -m 755 kubeseal-$GOOS-$GOARCH /usr/local/bin/kubeseal
```

Then create the SealedSecret CRD and launch the controller:

```
$ kubectl create -f https://github.com/bitnami/sealed-secrets/releases/
            download/v0.5.1/sealedsecret-crd.yaml

$ kubectl create -f https://github.com/bitnami/sealed-secrets/releases/
            download/v0.5.1/controller.yaml
```

The result will be that you have a new custom resource and a new pod running in the kube-system namespace:

```
$ kubectl get customresourcedefinitions
NAME                            AGE
sealedsecrets.bitnami.com    34s

$ kubectl get pods -n kube-system | grep sealed
sealed-secrets-controller-867944df58-l74nk    1/1        Running   0        38s
```

You are now ready to start using sealed-secrets. First, generate a generic secret manifest:

```
$ kubectl create secret generic oreilly --from-literal=password=root -o json
                                    --dry-run > secret.json

$ cat secret.json
{
    "kind": "Secret",
    "apiVersion": "v1",
    "metadata": {
        "name": "oreilly",
        "creationTimestamp": null
    },
    "data": {
        "password": "cm9vdA=="
    }
}
```

 To create a manifest but not create the object on the API server, use the --dry-run option. This will print your manifest to stdout. If you want YAML, use the -o yaml option; and if you want JSON, use -o json.

Then use the kubeseal command to generate the new custom SealedSecret object:

```
$ kubeseal < secret.json > sealedsecret.json

$ cat sealedsecret.json
{
  "kind": "SealedSecret",
  "apiVersion": "bitnami.com/v1alpha1",
  "metadata": {
    "name": "oreilly",
    "namespace": "default",
    "creationTimestamp": null
  },
  "spec": {
    "data": "AgDXiFG0V6NKF8e9k1NeBMc5t4QmfZh3QKuDORAsFNCt50wTwRhRLRAQOnz0sDk..."
  }
}
```

You can now store *sealedsecret.json* safely in version control. Only the private key stored in the sealed-secret controller can decrypt it. Once you create the `SealedSe cret` object, the controller will detect it, decrypt it, and generate the corresponding secret:

```
$ kubectl create -f sealedsecret.json
sealedsecret "oreilly" created

$ kubectl get sealedsecret
NAME     AGE
oreilly  5s

$ kubectl get secrets
NAME       TYPE    DATA   AGE
...
oreilly    Opaque  1      5s
```

See Also

- The sealed-secrets repository (*https://github.com/bitnami/sealed-secrets*)
- Angus Lees's article "Sealed Secrets: Protecting Your Passwords Before They Reach Kubernetes" (*https://engineering.bitnami.com/articles/sealed-secrets.html*)

14.7 Deploying Functions with kubeless

Problem

You want to deploy Python, Node.js, Ruby, or PowerShell functions to Kubernetes without having to build a Docker container. You also want to be able to call those functions via HTTP or by sending events to a message bus.

Solution

Use the Kubernetes-native serverless solution `kubeless`.

`kubeless` uses a `CustomResourceDefinition` (see Recipe 13.4) to define `Function` objects and a controller to deploy these functions inside pods within a Kubernetes cluster.

While the possibilities are quite advanced, in this recipe we will show a basic example of deploying a Python function that returns the JSON payload you send it.

First, create a `kubeless` namespace and launch the controller. To do so, you can get the manifest that is released with every version on the GitHub release page (*https://github.com/kubeless/kubeless/releases*). From that same release page, also download the `kubeless` binary:

```
$ kubectl create ns kubeless

$ curl -sL https://github.com/kubeless/kubeless/releases/download/v0.3.1/ \
    kubeless-rbac-v0.3.1.yaml | kubectl create -f -

$ wget https://github.com/kubeless/kubeless/releases/download/v0.3.1/ \
    kubeless_darwin-amd64.zip

$ sudo cp bundles/kubeless_darwin-amd64/kubeless /usr/local/bin
```

Within the kubeless namespace, you will see three pods: the controller that watches the Function custom endpoints, and the Kafka and Zookeeper pods. The latter two pods are only needed for functions that are triggered by events. For HTTP-triggered functions, you only need the controller to be in the running state:

```
$ kubectl get pods -n kubeless
NAME                                 READY   STATUS    RESTARTS   AGE
kafka-0                              1/1     Running   0          6m
kubeless-controller-9bff848c4-gnl7d  1/1     Running   0          6m
zoo-0                                1/1     Running   0          6m
```

To try kubeless, write the following Python function in a file called *post.py*:

```
def handler(context):
    print context.json
    return context.json
```

You can then deploy this function in Kubernetes using the kubeless CLI. The function deploy command takes several optional arguments. The --runtime option specifies what language the function is written in; the --http-trigger option specifies that the function will be triggered via HTTP(S) calls; and the --handler option specifies the name of the function, with the prefix being the basename of the file the function is stored in. Finally, the --from-file option specifies the file in which the function is written:

```
$ kubeless function deploy post-python --trigger-http \
                            --runtime python2.7 \
                            --handler post.handler \
                            --from-file post.py
INFO[0000] Deploying function...
INFO[0000] Function post-python submitted for deployment
INFO[0000] Check the deployment status executing 'kubeless function ls post-python'

$ kubeless function ls
NAME          NAMESPACE   HANDLER               RUNTIME   TYPE   TOPIC
post-python   default     hellowithdata.handler python    2.7    HTTP

$ kubectl get pods
NAME                          READY   STATUS    RESTARTS   AGE
post-python-5bcb9f7d86-d7nbt  1/1     Running   0          6s
```

The kubeless controller detected the new `Function` object and created a deployment for it. The function code is stored in a config map (see Recipe 8.3) and injected into the running pod at runtime. Then the function is callable via HTTP. The following shows these few objects:

```
$ kubectl get functions
NAME          AGE
post-python   2m

$ kubectl get cm
NAME          DATA   AGE
post-python   3      2m

$ kubectl get deployments
NAME          DESIRED   CURRENT   UP-TO-DATE   AVAILABLE   AGE
post-python   1         1         1            1           2m
```

To call the function you can use the `kubeless function call` command, like so:

```
$ kubeless function call post-python --data '{"oreilly":"function"}'
{"oreilly": "function"}
```

> kubeless can be used for much more than basic HTTP-triggered functions. Use the `--help` option to explore the CLI: `kubeless --help`.

See Also

- The kubeless repository (*https://github.com/kubeless/kubeless*)

- kubeless examples (*https://github.com/kubeless/kubeless/tree/master/examples*)

- Kubeless on Azure Container Services (*https://github.com/kubeless/kubeless/blob/master/docs/kubeless-on-azure-container-services.md*)

Resources

General

- Kubernetes Documentation (*https://kubernetes.io/docs/home/*)
- Kubernetes GitHub repository (*https://github.com/kubernetes/kubernetes/*)
- The Kubernetes community on GitHub (*https://github.com/kubernetes/commu nity/*)

Tutorials and Examples

- Kubernetes by Example (*http://kubernetesbyexample.com*)
- The Katacoda Kubernetes playground (*https://www.katacoda.com/courses/kuber netes/playground*)
- *Kubernetes: Up and Running* (*http://shop.oreilly.com/product/0636920043874.do*), by Brendan Burns, Kelsey Hightower, and Joe Beda (O'Reilly)

Index

A

access control
    for resources, 103-105
    listing and viewing information on, 99-103
administrator roles, 109
annotations (resource), 61
API groups, 55, 143
API server, 16, 32
apiVersion field, 55
application-level scaling, 89
applications, installing with Helm, 150
authorization
    role-based access control, 99-103
autocompletion for kubectl, 125
autoscalers, 89
    AWS Cluster, 93
    GKE Cluster, 90-93
    Horizontal Pod Autoscaler, 94-96
AWS
    automatically resizing cluster in, 93
    creating Kubernetes cluster with kubicorn, 154-158
az CLI, 22
Azure Cloud Shell, 25
Azure Container Service (ACS)
    creating a Kubernetes cluster on, 22

B

bash, xii, 125
batch jobs, 63-65

C

cascading versus direct deletion, 29
client and server binaries, downloading, 14

cluster scaling, 89
    automatically resizing a cluster in GKE, 90-93
ClusterIP type, 46
    accessing ClusterIP service outside the cluster, 127
clusters
    adding worker node to, 135
    creating with kubicorn, 154-159
    exploring roles in, 101
    getting detailed snapshot of state, 134
code examples from this book, xiii
command-line interface (kubectl) (see kubectl)
command-line interface (minikube), 5
config maps, 79-80
    creating for Prometheus, 117
containers
    accessing logs, 109
    exchanging data between, via local volume, 73
    in pod manifest, 35
    installing container runtime, 136
    liveness and readiness probes defined in, 113
CPU utilization, 89
CronJob object, 65
custom resource definition (CRD), 144-147, 161
    deletion with kubectl, 29

D

DaemonSet object, 66, 138
dashboard (Kubernetes), accessing from Minikube, 6

adding to deployments, 112-114
LoadBalancer type, 48
logging, 109
    (see also monitoring and logging)
    using Elasticsearch-Fluentd-Kibana (EFK),
        121-124
logstash, 124

M
maintenance
    draining Kubernetes node for, 137-139
    managing etcd, 139-140
manifests
    converting Docker compose files to, 153
    creating objects from, 34
    defining labels in, 60
    for Prometheus app, 118
    for services, 44
    for StatefulSets, 67
    in this book, GitHub repository, xiii
    Ingress object, 49
    launching a deployment with, 36-40
    structure of, 55
    writing for a batch job, 63
    writing for CronJobs, 65
    writing for DaemonSet, 66
    writing for pods, 35
    writing to create namespaces, 57
metadata field, 55
Minikube
    accessing Kubernetes dashboard, 6
    deploying ingress controller on, 48
    enabling Heapster to monitor resources,
        115-116
    installing to run local Kubernetes instance, 3
    kubectl installation, 3
    starting your first application on, 6
    understanding data persistency on, 84-87
    using a persistent volume with, 81-84
    using Elasticsearch-Fluentd-Kibana (EFK)
        on, 121-124
    using locally for Kubernetes development, 5
    using Prometheus on, 116-121
minikube version command, 4
monitoring and logging, 109-124
    accessing logs of a container, 109
    adding liveness and readiness probes to
        deployments, 112-114

controlling traffic flow to pods using readi-
    ness probes, 111
enabling Heapster on Minikube to monitor
    resources, 115-116
recovery using liveness probes, 110
using Elasticsearch-Fluentd-Kibana (EFK)
    on Minikube, 121-124
using Prometheus on Minikube, 116-121

N
namespace
    creating using a YAML manifest, 34
namespaces
    creating to avoid name collisions, 56
    deleting all pods in, using kubectl, 29
    deleting all resources in, using kubectl, 28
    listing roles available in, 100
    persistent volume claims in, 84
    secrets in, 77
    setting quotas in, 57
Network File System (NFS), 84
network, creating for Kubernetes cluster, 13
nodes
    adding worker node, 135
    draining for maintenance, 137-139
    running infrastructure daemons per node,
        66
non-cloud native apps, 70

O
OODA loop, 131

P
package management, xiii
package manager (Kubernetes) (see Helm)
passphrase, 75
persistent volume claim, 82, 84-87
persistent volumes, 81-84
    dynamically provisioning on GKE, 87
PetSet, 70
PHP app, 94
playground (Kubernetes), 1
pod security policies, 106
pods
    controlling traffic flow using readiness
        probes, 111
    debugging, 130-134
    deleting using kubectl, 29

influencing startup behavior, 71
removing from a service, 126
running a scheduled job in, 65
scaling, 89
    (see also scaling)
securing, 106
service account in, 98
supervision by deployment, 38
watching with kubectl, 29
writing a manifest from scratch, 35
probes, 114
    (see also liveness probes; readiness probes)
Prometheus, 116-121
proxies
    running with kubectrl, 45
Python, xiii
    client for Kubernetes, 143

Q

quality of service (QoS) class, 129
queries, using labels for, 59
quotas for resources in a namespace, 57

R

readiness probes, 111
    adding to deployments, 112-114
Redis, 150
    dashboard view of application, 7
regions (Azure), 23
replica sets (RSs), 38
ReplicaSet object, 36
resourcces
    custom resource definition, 161
resource groups (Azure), 22
    deleting, 25
ResourceQuota object, 57
resources
    access control for, 103-105
    annotating, 61
    changes in, watching with kubectl, 29
    custom resource definition, 144-147
    deleting with kubectl, 28
    editing with kubectl, 30
    explaining using kubectl, 30
    listing, 27
    short names for, 28
    understanding and parsing statuses, 128-130
restart policy, 114

role-based access control (RBAC), 100-103
    setting up for Prometheus, 117

S

scaling, 89-96
    a deployment, 89
    automatically resizing AWS cluster, 93
    automatically resizing GKE cluster, 90-93
    using horizontal pod autoscaling in GKE, 94-96
schedule section (manifests), 65
SealedSecret object, 159-161
secrets
    encrypted, storing in version control, 159-161
    passing API access key to a pod via, 75-79
security, 97-107
    access control for resources, 103-105
    access control information, listing and viewing, 99-103
    defining security context for pods, 106
    unique identity for an application, 97-99
selector, 45
    using to query objects, 59
service accounts, 97
    creating for Prometheus, 118
Service object, creating, 44
    writing YAML file for, 45
services, 43-52
    changing service type, 46-48
    concept of, 44
    creating to expose your application, 44-45
    deleting with kubectl, 29
    deploying ingress controller on Minikube, 48
    listing endpoints, 129
    listing services and deployments with kubectl, 27
    making accessible from outside the cluster, 49-52
    verifying DNS entry for, 46
SHA256 hash, verifying for Kubernetes release on GitHub, 14
spec field, 56
StatefulSet object, 67
status field, 56
storage classes (Minikube), 85
systemd, writing unit file to run Kubernetes components, 18

About the Authors

Sébastien Goasguen built his first compute cluster in the late '90s and takes pride in having completed his PhD thanks to Fortran 77 and partial differential equations. His struggles with parallel computers led him to work on making computing a utility and to focus on grids and, later, clouds. Fifteen years later, he secretly hopes that containers and Kubernetes will let him get back to writing applications.

He is currently the senior director of cloud technologies at Bitnami, where he leads the Kubernetes efforts. He founded Skippbox, a Kubernetes startup, in late 2015. While at Skippbox, he created several open source software applications and tools to enhance the user experience of Kubernetes. He is a member of the Apache Software Foundation and a former vice president of Apache CloudStack. Sébastien focuses on the cloud ecosystem and has contributed to dozens of open source projects. He is the author of the *Docker Cookbook*, an avid blogger, and an online instructor of Kubernetes concepts for Safari subscribers.

Michael Hausenblas is a developer advocate for Go, Kubernetes, and OpenShift at Red Hat, where he helps AppOps to build and operate distributed services. His background is in large-scale data processing and container orchestration and he's experienced in advocacy and standardization at W3C and IETF. Before Red Hat, Michael worked at Mesosphere, MapR, and two research institutions in Ireland and Austria. He contributes to open source software (mainly using Go), blogs, and hangs out on Twitter too much.

Colophon

The animal on the cover of *Kubernetes Cookbook* is a Bengal eagle owl *(Bubo bengalensis)*. These large horned owls are usually seen in pairs and can be found in hilly and rocky scrub forests throughout South Asia.

The Bengal eagle owl measures 19–22 inches tall and weighs between 39–70 ounces. Its feathers are brownish-gray or beige and its ears have brown tufts. In contrast to the neutral color of its body, its eye color is strikingly orange. Owls with orange eyes hunt during the day. It prefers a meaty diet and mostly feasts on rodents such as mice or rats but will also resort to eating other birds during the winter. This owl produces a deep, resonant, booming, two-note "whooo" call that can be heard at dusk and dawn.

Females build nests in shallow recesses in the ground, rock ledges, and river banks, and lay 2–5 cream colored eggs. The eggs hatch after 33 days. By the time the chicks are around 10 weeks of age, they are adult-sized, though not mature yet, and they depend on their parents for nearly six months. To distract predators from their offspring, the parents will pretend to have a wing injury or fly in a zigzag manner.

Many of the animals on O'Reilly covers are endangered; all of them are important to the world. To learn more about how you can help, go to *animals.oreilly.com*.

The cover image is from *Meyers Kleines Lexicon*. The cover fonts are URW Typewriter and Guardian Sans. The text font is Adobe Minion Pro; the heading font is Adobe Myriad Condensed; and the code font is Dalton Maag's Ubuntu Mono.